BOWSTEAD AND REYNOLDS

ON

AGENCY

VOLUMES IN THE COMMON LAW LIBRARY

THE COMMON LAW LIBRARY

BOWSTEAD AND REYNOLDS

ON

AGENCY

FIRST SUPPLEMENT TO THE TWENTY-SECOND EDITION

BY

PETER WATTS QC, LLM (Cantab), FRSNZ

Senior Research Fellow, Harris Manchester College, Oxford
GENERAL EDITOR

AND

F.M.B. REYNOLDS QC (Hon), DCL, FBA

Honorary Bencher of the Inner Temple; Professor of Law Emeritus in the
University of Oxford and Emeritus Fellow of Worcester College, Oxford

SWEET & MAXWELL  THOMSON REUTERS

Published in 2021 by Thomson Reuters, trading as Sweet & Maxwell.
Thomson Reuters is registered in England & Wales. Company number
1679046.
Registered Office and address for service: 5 Canada Square, Canary Wharf,
London, E14 5AQ.

For further information on our products and services, visit *http://
www.sweetandmaxwell.co.uk.*

Computerset by Sweet & Maxwell.
Printed and bound by CPI Group (UK) Ltd, Croydon, CR0 4YY.
A CIP catalogue record for this book is available from the British Library.

ISBN (print): 978-0-414-09883-1

ISBN (e-book): 978-0-414-09885-5

ISBN (print and ebook): 978-0-414-09884-8

Thomson Reuters, the Thomson Reuters Logo and Sweet & Maxwell ® are
trademarks of Thomson Reuters.

HOW TO USE THIS SUPPLEMENT

This is the First Supplement to the Twenty-second Edition of *Bowstead & Reynolds on Agency*, and has been compiled according to the structure of the main work.

At the beginning of each chapter of this Supplement, a mini table of contents has been included. Where a heading in this table of contents has been marked with a square pointer, this indicates that there is relevant information in the Supplement to which the reader should refer. Within each chapter, updating information is referenced to the relevant paragraph in the main work.

PREFACE

This First Supplement to the Twenty-second Edition covers material up to the end of July 2021. All chapters other than Chapter 4 have acquired some annotation. As usual, the annotations attempt to be fairly comprehensive of England & Wales case law (omitting cases that are entirely routine). A list of new England and Wales cases is set out below. Otherwise, useful recent authorities from Australia, New Zealand, and Singapore are included. An opportunity has also been taken to add some, mainly brief, revisions to the body of the text on a range of topics, including: the liability of parent companies for the conduct of businesses of subsidiaries in the light of *Okpabi v Royal Dutch Shell Plc* [2021] UKSC 3; ministerial agents; the circumstances in which an agent can be said to be acting for both parties, and the operation of the no-inhibition principle where an agent is so acting; the role of liquidator in giving consent to what would otherwise be a breach of fiduciary duty; the relevance of the cause of action to the imputation of an agent's knowledge; the ability of a principal to sue an agent in order to cure a liability incurred to a third party; and the circumstances in which an agent might be liable in knowing receipt in respect of the agent's remuneration.

Chapter 1: Advisor or agent?; agency involving companies; agency and sale; ministerial agents. *Wood v Commercial First Business Ltd* [2021] EWCA Civ 471; [2021] 3 W.L.R. 395; *Tattersalls Ltd v McMahon* [2021] EWHC 1629 (QB); *Satyam Enterprises Ltd v Burton* [2021] EWCA Civ 287; *Tuke v Hood* [2020] EWHC 2843 (Comm); *Cameron v Cameron* [2021] EWHC 229 (Ch).

Chapter 2: Identifying party for whom agent acts; requirements as to form when agent signs for principal. *NDH Properties Ltd v Lupton Fawcett LLP* [2020] EWHC 3056 (Ch); *Prempeh v Lakhany* [2020] EWCA Civ 1422.

Chapter 3: Lack of authority and arbitration clauses. *Republic of Mozambique v Credit Suisse International* [2021] EWCA Civ 329.

Chapter 5: Sub-agency and co-owners. *Sotheby's v Mark Weiss Ltd* [2020] EWCA Civ 1570.

Chapter 6: Duties of care and skill; conflict of interest; trust of assets in possession of agent; account of profits; misuse of confidential information; bribes and secret commissions. *Sciortino v Beaumont* [2021] EWCA Civ 786; [2021] 3 W.L.R. 343; *Bishopsgate Contracting Solutions Ltd v O'Sullivan* [2021] EWHC 2103 (QB); *Lennon v Englefield* [2021] EWHC 1473 (QB); *Secretariat Consulting Pte Ltd v A Company* [2021] EWCA Civ 6; [2001] 4 W.L.R. 20; *Fairford Water Ski Club Ltd v Cohoon* [2021] EWCA Civ 143; *Barrowfen Properties Ltd v Patel* [2021] EWHC 2055 (Ch); *National Stadium Project (Grenada) Corp v NH International (Caribbean) Ltd* [2020] UKPC 25; *Gray v Global Energy Horizons Corp* [2020] EWCA Civ 1668; [2021] 1 W.L.R. 2264; *Langer v McKeown* [2020] EWHC 3485 (Ch); *Lifestyle Equities CV v Ahmed* [2021] EWCA Civ 675; [2021] Bus L.R. 1020; *Travel Counsellors Ltd v Trailfinders Ltd* [2021] EWCA Civ 38; *Kings Security Systems Ltd v King* [2021] EWHC 325 (Ch); *Wood v Commercial First Business Ltd* [2021] EWCA Civ 471; [2021] 3 W.L.R. 395.

Chapter 7: Solicitor's remuneration; effective cause requirements in commission contracts; solicitor's lien. *Belsner v Cam Legal Services Ltd* [2020] EWHC 2755 (QB); *Cakebread v Fitzwilliam* [2021] EWHC 472 (Comm); *EMFC Loan Syndications LLP v The Resort Group Plc* [2021] EWCA Civ 844; *Winlink*

Marketing Ltd v The Liverpool Football Club & Athletic Grounds Ltd [2020]
EWHC 2271 (Comm); *Serious Fraud Office v Litigation Capital Ltd* [2021]
EWHC 1272 (Comm).

Chapter 8: Determining whether principal or agent party to contract; holding
out in apparent authority; relevance of agency law to estoppel; election; vicarious
liability; parent company liability; imputation of an agent's knowledge. *Gregor
Fisken Ltd v Carl* [2021] EWCA Civ 792; [2021] 4 W.L.R. 91; *Bell v Ivy Technology Ltd* [2020] EWCA Civ 1563; *Sotheby's v Mark Weiss Ltd* [2020] EWCA Civ
1570; *Active Media Services Inc v Burmester, Duncker & Joly GmbH & Co Kg*
[2021] EWHC 232 (Comm); *Barry Congregation of Jehovah's Witnesses v BXB*
[2021] EWCA Civ 356; [2021] 4 W.L.R. 42; *Natwest Markets Plc v Bilta (UK)
Ltd* [2021] EWCA Civ 680; *Okpabi v Royal Dutch Shell Plc* [2021] UKSC 3;
[2021] 1 W.L.R. 1294.

Chapter 9: Liability of company director bidding at auction; effect of agent
signing contract without signalling agency status; agent's liability in negligent
misstatement; liability for procuring or participating in tort; liability of agent in
dishonest assistance; liability of agents for remuneration earned helping principal
defend breach of trust allegation. *Tattersalls Ltd v McMahon* [2021] EWHC 1629
(QB); *Gregor Fisken Ltd v Carl* [2021] EWCA Civ 792; [2021] 4 W.L.R. 91;
NDH Properties Ltd v Lupton Fawcett LLP [2020] EWHC 3056 (Ch); *Barclay-
Watt v Alpha Panareti Public Ltd* [2021] EWHC 1327 (Comm); *PJSC Uralkali v
Rowley* [2020] EWHC 3442 (Ch); *Lifestyle Equities CV v Ahmed* [2021] EWCA
Civ 675; [2021] Bus L.R. 1020; *Tunein Inc v Warner Music UK Ltd* [2021] EWCA
Civ 441; *Natwest Markets Plc v Bilta (UK) Ltd* [2021] EWCA Civ 680; *Uavend
Properties Inc v Adsaax Ltd* [2020] EWHC 2073 (Comm); *Re Smith; Serious
Fraud Office v Litigation Capital Ltd* [2021] EWHC 1272 (Comm); *London
Capital & Finance Plc v Thomson* [2021] EWHC 1833 (Ch).

Chapter 10: Implied termination and successive powers of attorney; withdraw-
ing agent's authority will not necessarily affect the operation of the existing
contractual rights of third parties. *Barclays Bank Plc v Al Saud* [2021] EWHC 701
(Comm).

Peter Watts
Bankside Chambers, Auckland, and Fountain Court Chambers, London
5 October 2021

STANDARD ABBREVIATIONS

Commonwealth Case Law Abbreviations

The citations to cases from the United Kingdom use standard abbreviations, which it is not necessary to set out herein. However, it may be useful for the reader to have an explanation of some of those used for Commonwealth cases. All recent Australian and New Zealand cases that are cited are available free at *http://www.austlii.edu.au*. Many Singapore cases are available free at *http://www.commonlii.org/* and Hong Kong cases at *https://www.hklii.hk/eng/*. Abbreviations with points refer to report series; those without are neutral citations.

A.C.L.C.	Australian Company Law Cases
A.C.S.R.	Australian Company and Securities Reports
ACTCA	Australian Capital Territory Court of Appeal
A.L.R.	Australian Law Reports
A.T.R.	Australian Tax Reports
A.N.Z. Conv.R.	Australian and New Zealand Conveyancing Reports
BCCA	British Columbia Court of Appeal
B.P.R.	Butterworths Property Reports
C.L.R.	Commonwealth Law Reports
D.L.R.	Dominion Law Reports
FCAFC	Federal Court of Australia Full Court
F.C.R.	Federal Court Reports
F.L.R.	Federal Law Reports
G.L.R.	Gazette Law Reports (New Zealand)
HCA	High Court of Australia
HKCA	Hong Kong Court of Appeal
H.K.C.F.A.R.	Hong Kong Court of Final Appeal Reports
HKCFI	Hong Kong Court of First Instance
HKCU	Hong Kong Cases Unreported
H.K.L.R.	Hong Kong Law Reports
H.K.L.R.D.	Hong Kong Law Reports & Digest
NSCA	Nova Scotia Court of Appeal
NSWCA	New South Wales Court of Appeal
NSWSC	New South Wales Supreme Court
N.Z.C.L.C.	New Zealand Company Law Cases
N.Z.C.P.R.	New Zealand Conveyancing and Property Reports
NZHC	New Zealand High Court
NZCA	New Zealand Court of Appeal
N.Z.L.R.	New Zealand Law Reports

NZSC	New Zealand Supreme Court
P.R.N.Z.	Procedure Reports of New Zealand
QCA	Queensland Court of Appeal
QSC	Queensland Supreme Court
SCC	Supreme Court of Canada
SGCA	Singapore Court of Appeal
SGHC	Singapore High Court
S.L.R.	Singapore Law Reports
V.R.	Victorian Reports
VSC	Supreme Court of Victoria
VSCA	Court of Appeal of Victoria
W.A.R.	Western Australia Reports

TABLE OF CONTENTS

TABLE OF CASES

INTERNATIONAL CASES

AUSTRALIA

CANADA

HONG KONG

IRELAND

NEW ZEALAND

SINGAPORE

SOUTH AFRICA

TABLE OF STATUTES

TABLE OF STATUTORY INSTRUMENTS

CHAPTER 1

NATURE OF THE SUBJECT

COMMENT

1. Theoretical basis of agency in the common law

Affecting principal's relations with third parties

Replace the third paragraph with:

Conversely, where there is no conferral of authority to alter legal relations, but **1-004** merely a chain of contracts, the intermediate contracting parties will not normally be agents and will not routinely owe fiduciary duties up the chain.[14] Equally, the mere fact that one person does something in order to benefit another, and the latter is relying on the former to do so or may have requested or even contracted for performance of the action, does not make the former the agent of the latter.[15] So too a non-owner of property, with or without the owner's consent, can contract to sell it or to have it repaired or improved without necessarily being the agent of the owner.[16] Nor does the fact that a third party, X, pays the remuneration of Y make Y the agent of X if Y is properly the agent of Z.[17] It is quite common (and not improper if assented to by the principal) for an agent's remuneration to be paid by the third party or some other person. More generally, mere economic interdependence between two parties does not create one the agent of the other.[18]

[14] See *Garnac Grain Co Inc v HMF Faure & Fairclough Ltd* [1968] A.C. 1130; and *Dinglis Management Ltd v Dinglis Properties Ltd* [2019] EWCA Civ 127.

[15] *Tonto Home Loans Australia Pty Ltd v Tavares* [2011] NSWCA 389 at [175]: "it is to be borne in mind that the concept of agency is not merely functional, whereby something that is necessary to be done for P and that could be done by P itself is done by A under some arrangement; rather it is a consensual arrangement, a relationship, whereby A is to be taken as, or as representing, P"; *London Borough of Haringey v Ahmed* [2017] EWCA Civ 1861 at [36]–[38] (husband not agent in procuring rented accommodation for wife and family); *Marme Inversiones 2007 SL v Natwest Markets Plc* [2019] EWHC 366 (Comm) at [444] (lead arranging bank not acting as agent for other banks in putting together syndicated financing); *Ventra Investments Ltd v Bank of Scotland Plc* [2019] EWHC 2058 (Comm) at [88]–[89] (bank-appointed adviser to receivers not agent of bank); *Zedra Trust Co (Jersey) Ltd v The Hut Group Ltd* [2019] EWHC 2191 (Comm) at [37] (contractual requirement that, if requested by X, Y commission independent report at expense of X does not make Y the agent of X); *Barness v Ingenious Media Ltd* [2019] EWHC 3299 (Ch) at [83] (banks as lenders into tax-driven scheme not principals of promoters of the scheme); *National Bank of Kazakhstan the Republic of Kazakhstan v Bank of New York Mellon SA/NV* [2020] EWHC 916 (Comm); [2020] 2 B.C.L.C. 726 at [87] (state bank not agent of state government).

[16] See *Foster v Action Aviation Ltd* [2014] EWCA Civ 1368 at [38]; and the other cases collected in

para.8–002, below. cf. *The Swan* [1968] 1 Lloyd's Rep. 5; Article 98, Illustration 6; *Sotheby's v Mark Weiss Ltd* [2020] EWCA Civ 1570 (one co-owner found agent of other in sale); *Bell v Ivy Technology Ltd* [2020] EWCA Civ 1563 (argument beneficial co-owner proper party to contract).

[17] See *Plevin v Paragon Personal Finance Ltd* [2014] UKSC 61; [2014] 1 W.L.R. 4222 at [33]. A solicitor paid for by an insurer to represent the insured in litigation is usually the agent of the insured, not the insurer: see *Groom v Crocker* [1939] 1 K.B. 194 at 227–228; *Travelers Insurance Co Ltd v XYZ* [2019] UKSC 48 at [114].

[18] See *Tonto Home Loans Australia Pty Ltd v Tavares* [2011] NSWCA 389 at [194]–[196]; *UBS AG (London Branch) v Kommunale Wasserwerke Leipzig GmbH* [2017] EWCA Civ 1567 at [100] (noted P. Kelshiker (2018) 134 L.Q.R. 363); *London Borough of Haringey v Ahmed* [2017] EWCA Civ 1861 at [38].

Replace the fifth paragraph with:

The centrality to agency of the conferral of authority to alter legal relations suggests that at common law being an agent is not a status, but a description of a person while and only so long as the person is exercising such authority. As to status, an agent's status will usually be that of employee or independent contractor (but sometimes a gratuitous actor), and agency is not a separate category. Equally, employees and contractors often have no authority to alter their appointer's legal relations, and if not exercising any authority are not properly described as an agent. Thus, a solicitor is usually a type of independent contractor, and when merely giving advice to a client is not an agent, but while acting for the client in communicating with outside parties would be an agent.[19a] An employee while formally on sick leave remains an employee but would not have actual authority as agent during the leave.[20] One of the implications of this is that agency is of limited utility in the application of vicarious liability in tort, which usually operates on the basis of a party's status.[21] On the other hand, advisers will often owe fiduciary duties, even though they are not agents in the standard sense of the term.[21a]

[19a] See *Wood v Commercial First Business Ltd* [2021] EWCA Civ 471; [2021] 3 W.L.R. 395 at [67].

[20] See *Harrisons & Crosfield Ltd v L & NW Ry Co Ltd* [1917] 2 K.B. 755.

[21] See below, paras 8-177 and 8-182.

[21a] See below, para.1-020.

Not an imposed relationship

Replace footnote 37 with:

1-007

[37] See *Good v Bruce* [1917] N.Z.L.R. 514 (CA) at 536 (agency not sale): "No doubt acts are sometimes more potent than words, but if the acts are dubious then the words are the more important"; *Pengelly v Business Mortgage Finance 4 Plc* [2020] EWHC 2002 (Ch) at [68] (affd *Wood v Commercial First Business Ltd* [2021] EWCA Civ 471; [2021] 3 W.L.R. 395 on different points).

Incomplete agency: internal relationship only—the "canvassing" or "introducing" agent

Replace footnote 69 with:

1-020

[69] See *Shipway v Broadwood* [1899] 1 Q.B. 369 (veterinarian to certify as to soundness of horses); *Alexander v Webber* [1922] 1 K.B. 642 (chauffeur to approve of car to be bought); *Taylor v Walker* [1958] 1 Lloyd's Rep. 490 (accident assessor). See too the discussion in *Wood v Commercial First Business Ltd* [2021] EWCA Civ 471; [2021] 3 W.L.R. 395 at [66].

Replace footnote 72 with:

[72] See *Medsted Associates Ltd v Canaccord Genuity Wealth (International) Ltd* [2019] EWCA Civ 83; [2019] 1 W.L.R. 4481 at [32] (introducer to main agent had fiduciary relationship with client, albeit limited). See too *Rowland v Chapman* (1901) 17 TLR 669 (agent who was also co-principal had no real conflict of interest).

Replace footnote 73 with:

[73] See *Pengelly v Business Mortgage Finance 4 Plc* [2020] EWHC 2002 (Ch) at [68] (affd *Wood v Commercial First Business Ltd* [2021] EWCA Civ 471; [2021] 3 W.L.R. 395 on other points).

Meaning of term "agent", where a question of construction

Replace paragraph with:

When it is necessary, as in statutory interpretation or in the construction of an **1-023** agreement, to attribute a meaning to the word "agent", it may be said that the central significance of the term agent refers to a person who attracts both the external and internal aspects of agency, for it is here that the complete complex of rules is most fully worked out, and it is because of the external powers that the internal duties are imposed. And where the term agent is used in a statute or formal document, it has been said that it may be presumed that the word is used in this, its proper legal connotation, unless there are strong contrary indications.[101] But there is certainly no rule to that effect, and the term is often used of any form of intermediary, or of persons who simply perform functions for others.[102] Conversely, the context may suggest that the word encompasses only professional agents who are independent contractors.[103] Similarly, the word "authority" in a statute may not require actual authorisation by the principal, but extend to acts, authorised or not, occurring in the performance of authorised tasks.[104] Another common form of words comes from the context of injunctions, which are often issued against "the defendant, its servant and agents". The only direct party will be the defendant, but the wording signals that the defendant needs to control those whom it has engaged to do the enjoined activity, who might be independent contractors that are not exercising any agency functions in the common law sense.[105]

[101] *Shell Co of Australia Ltd v Nat Shipping and Bagging Services Ltd (The Kilmun)* [1988] 2 Lloyd's Rep. 1 at 16, per Sir Denys Buckley (in a dissenting judgment); *Canada v Merchant Law Group* 2010 FCA 206 (Can. Fed. CA) at [17] (incidence of goods and services tax); *Plevin v Paragon Personal Finance Ltd* [2014] UKSC 61; [2014] 1 W.L.R. 4222 at [30]; *Guan v Lui* [2021] NSWCA 65 (mere introducer not within licensing regime).

[102] See, e.g. *Laemthong International Lines Co Ltd v Artis (The Laemthong Glory)* [2005] EWCA Civ 519; [2005] 1 Lloyd's Rep. 688 (promise to indemnify "you, your servants or agents" considered in the context of the Contracts (Rights of Third Parties) Act 1999: shipowner held "agent" of charterer for delivering cargo and so able to sue). Another example is the reference to "servants or agents" in Art.IV bis 2 of the Hague-Visby Rules scheduled to the Carriage of Goods by Sea Act 1971: see *Carver on Bills of Lading* (4th edn), para.9-303. See further *The Happy Day* [2002] EWCA Civ 1068; [2002] 2 Lloyd's Rep. 487 (agency of receiver for charterer); *Commerce Commission v Vero Insurance New Zealand Ltd* (2006) 8 N.Z.C.L.C. 101, 871 (possession of apparent authority enough to meet the operative provision of a statute that a person be an agent); *Commissioners for Revenue and Customs v Insurancewide.Com Services Ltd* [2010] EWCA Civ 422; [2010] S.T.C. 1572 at [87] (exemption from VAT for insurance brokers and agents); *Revenue and Customs v Secret Hotels2 Ltd* [2014] UKSC 16; [2014] S.T.C. 937 (VAT intermediaries); *Actavis Group hf v Eli Lilly & Co* [2013] EWCA Civ 517; [2013] R.P.C. 37 at [57] (business carried on through an agent); *NYK Bulkship (Atlantic) NV v Cargill International SA* [2016] UKSC 20; [2016] 1 W.L.R. 1853, discussed in F.M.B. Reynolds and C.H. Tan [2018] Sing J.L.S. 43, 54 (only irrelevant functions of sub-charterers were those of "agent" and otherwise they were independent parties).

[103] See, e.g. *Public Prosecutor v Lam Leng Hung* [2018] SGCA 7 at [125]. cf. *Tattersalls Ltd v McMahon* [2021] EWHC 1629 (QB) (auction contract referring to "agents" captures director).

[104] See *Kemeh v Ministry of Defence* [2014] EWCA Civ 91; [2014] I.C.R. 625 at [11] (racial discrimination). See too *Unite the Union v Nailard* [2018] EWCA Civ 1203; [2019] I.C.R. 28.

[105] There is a useful discussion in *Kirkpatrick v Kotis* (2004) 62 N.S.W.L.R. 567 at [81]–[100].

2. Agency law and companies

Attributing acts, omissions and states of mind to companies

Replace footnote 157 with:

[157] *Tesco Supermarkets Ltd v Nattrass* [1972] A.C. 153 at 198–199; *Bilta (UK) Ltd v Nazir (No.2)* [2015] **1-028**

UKSC 23; [2016] A.C. 1 at [181] and [205], per Lords Toulson and Hodge; *Tattersalls Ltd v McMahon* [2021] EWHC 1629 (QB) at [27].

Replace footnote 171 with:

171 The concept of informal unanimous assent seems to have its origins in an implication into the deeds of partnerships: see *Const v Harris* (1824) T. & R. 496 at 522, per Lord Eldon LC; and *Re Vale of Neath and South Wales Brewery Co, Morgan's Case* (1849) 1 De G. & S. 750 at 776 (joint stock company). The assent need be only of voting shareholders: *Jackson v Dear* [2012] EWHC 2060 (Ch) at [68]; reversed on other issues [2013] EWCA Civ 89; [2014] 1 B.C.L.C. 186. Difficult issues arise, however, where the assent is only of the beneficial owner of shares. If the legal owner has delegated particular, or all, decision-making to the beneficial owner, then the latter is likely to have authority to bind the former: see Watts (2006) 122 L.Q.R. 15; and *Ciban Management Corp v Citco (BVI) Ltd* [2020] UKPC 21; [2020] 3 W.L.R. 705 at [47] (noted Watts (2021) 137 L.Q.R. 20).

Replace footnote 176 with:

176 *Re New Cedos Engineering Co Ltd* [1994] 1 B.C.L.C. 797 at 814; *Madoff Securities International Ltd v Raven* [2011] EWHC 3102 (Comm) at [111] (no shareholder ratification of fraud); *Satyam Enterprises Ltd v Burton* [2021] EWCA Civ 287 at [47] (unlawful return of capital).

Agency of companies for each other or for shareholders

Replace paragraph with:

1-030   It may appear tempting to regard a subsidiary company as agent for the principal company; or even the principal as agent for the subsidiary. This would have the effect of circumventing (rather than piercing) the corporate veil. English courts have not looked favourably on such arguments, and situations where there is such agency would be required to be proved by normal criteria,[195] as where a trader converted his or her business into a limited company and it was specifically provided that the new company would perform sale contracts entered into by the previous company as agent for the vendor.[196] Similarly, courts will not lightly find that companies, or their directors, are agents for their human shareholders, but cases will arise where this is the correct conclusion.[197] Sometimes too the facts may support a conclusion that a director or employee of a parent company has authority, actual or apparent, to bind or otherwise act on behalf of a subsidiary, or vice versa.[198] Otherwise, it is recognised that:

"In commercial terms the creation of a corporate structure is by definition designed to create separate legal entities for entirely legitimate purposes which would often if not usually be defeated by any general agency relationship between them."[199]

It remains possible that a shareholder, including a parent company, may have done things in its own right that are sufficient to create a direct tortious liability.[200] In some circumstances it may be possible to show that a shareholder, including a parent company, has genuinely assumed legal responsibility for action that is found to be tortious. Torts involving pure economic loss are primary candidates for such an analysis. Questions of authority, and agency principles in general, may apply in such cases. However, in cases involving personal injury and damage to property, it is also possible for shareholders to become liable for negligence by reason of the mere degree to which they have involved themselves in the company's operations, or health and safety aspects of those operations, where injury took place. In such circumstances, attribution to a shareholder of the acts and knowledge of personnel acting for the shareholder probably does not turn on authority in the strict sense, but on concepts similar to those deployed for vicarious liability (even if liability is direct rather than vicarious). Otherwise, the question of when the corporate veil may be pierced is a matter for company law.[201]

195 See *Savill v Chase Holdings (Wellington) Ltd* [1989] 1 N.Z.L.R. 257 (CA, affirmed PC); *Adams v*

Cape Industries Plc [1990] Ch. 439 (doing business for purpose of jurisdiction as relevant to enforcement of foreign judgment); *Scriven v Scriven* [2015] EWHC 1690 (Ch) at [269]; *Dinglis Management Ltd v Dinglis Properties Ltd* [2019] EWCA Civ 127. See too *Telewest Communications Plc v Customs and Excise Commissioners* [2005] EWCA Civ 102; [2005] S.T.C. 481; *Premier Building and Consulting Pty Ltd v Spotless Group Ltd* (2008) 64 A.C.S.R. 114 at [339]. cf. *Globex Foreign Exchange Corp v Launt* 2011 NSCA 67.

[196] *Southern v Watson* [1940] 3 All E.R. 439. See also *Rainham Chemical Works Ltd v Belvedere Fish Guano Co Ltd* [1921] 2 A.C. 465 (newly formed company in possession of land as agent of the vendor); *Chief Executive of the New Zealand Customs Service v Nike New Zealand Ltd* [2004] 1 N.Z.L.R. 238 (parent company held buying agent of subsidiary); *Secretariat Consulting Pte Ltd v A Company* [2021] EWCA Civ 6; [2001] 4 W.L.R. 20 at [74].

[197] See *Prest v Petrodel Resources Ltd* [2013] UKSC 34; [2013] 2 A.C. 415 at [32]–[33]; explaining *Trustor AB v Smallbone (No.2)* [2001] 1 W.L.R. 1177; *Park's of Hamilton's (Holdings) Ltd v Campbell* [2014] CSIH 36; 2014 S.C. 726 (directors as negotiating agent for shareholders in takeover); *Wise v Jimenez* [2014] 1 P. & C.R. DG9 (company mere conduit for money provided by shareholder); *MDW Holdings Ltd v Norvill* [2021] EWHC 1135 (Ch) at [270] (no agency on part of company or directors in providing information to buyer of shares from shareholder).

[198] See, e.g. *Enron (Thrace) Exploration and Production BV v Clapp* [2005] EWHC 401 (Comm) at [92]; *Cromwell Corp Ltd v Sofrana Immobilier (NZ) Ltd* (1992) 6 N.Z.C.L.C. 67, 997; *HKSAR v Luk Kin* [2016] HKCFA 81 at [33]. A director who ceases to be an executive director of the parent company and moves to become an executive director of a subsidiary normally ceases to have actual authority to bind the parent, though apparent authority may linger: see *Benourad v Compass Group Plc* [2010] EWHC 1882 (QB) at [113]. See too *Hudson Bay Apparel Brands LLC v Umbro International Ltd* [2010] EWCA Civ 949; [2011] 1 B.C.L.C. 259 (managing director of subsidiary with authority to administer US licences had no authority on behalf of parent company to vary those licences); *London Executive Aviation Ltd v The Royal Bank of Scotland Plc* [2018] EWHC 74 (Ch) at [295] (employee of parent company, and possibly parent company itself, acting as agent of subsidiary).

[199] *Peterson Farms Inc v C&M Farming Ltd* [2004] EWHC 21 (Comm); [2004] 1 Lloyd's Rep. 603 at [62], per Langley J (arbitrators had awarded damages for "parent losses"). See also *The Coral Rose* [1991] 1 Lloyd's Rep. 563 (borrower not agent); *Yukong Lines v Rendsburg Investment Corp (The Rialto) (No.2)* [1998] 1 Lloyd's Rep. 322 ("owners" of company not undisclosed principals of company as named charterer); *IBM United Kingdom Holdings Ltd v Dalgleish* [2017] EWCA Civ 1212 at [372] (motives of senior employee of parent company not attributed to subsidiary). See also Harris (2005) 23 Coy & Securities, L.J. 7.

[200] *Chandler v Cape Plc* [2011] EWHC 951 (QB) at [75]; affd [2012] EWCA Civ 525; [2012] 1 W.L.R. 3111; *Strategic Formwork Pty Ltd v Hitchen* [2018] NSWCA 54; *Lungowe v Vedanta Resources Plc* [2019] UKSC 20; [2020] A.C. 1045 at [49]; *Okpabi v Royal Dutch Shell Plc* [2021] UKSC 3; [2021] 1 W.L.R. 1294.

[201] As to which see *Gower's Principles of Modern Company Law* (10th edn), p.197 onwards; and *Prest v Petrodel Resources Ltd* [2013] UKSC 34; [2013] 2 A.C. 415. Fiduciary duties, or duties in negligence, can sometimes be owed to the company or person "behind" a company: see *Johnson v Gore Wood & Co* [2002] 2 A.C. 1; *Ratiu v Conway* [2005] EWCA Civ 1302; cf. *Diamantis v JP Morgan Chase Bank* [2005] EWCA Civ 1612.

3. Agency distinguished from other relationships

Agent and trustee

Replace footnote 211 with:

[211] See further below, para.2-022. See, Watts, in *Equity, Trusts and Commerce* (Davies and Penner eds, 2017), Ch.2. Note that co-owners are not automatically agents of one another: see *Kennedy v De Trafford* [1897] A.C. 180 at 188; cf. *Sotheby's v Mark Weiss Ltd* [2020] EWCA Civ 1570.

1-032

Agent and seller; agent and buyer

Replace footnote 251 with:

[251] *Ex p. White, re Neville* (1871) L.R. 6 Ch.App. 397; *Jones v Southwark LBC* [2016] EWHC 457 (Ch) at [52]; *Tuke v Hood* [2020] EWHC 2843 (Comm) at [222].

1-036

COMMENT

Nuntius and other ministerial agents

Replace paragraph with:

Sometimes a person may be asked to undertake a specific task on behalf of a

1-047

principal under close direction of the principal and sometimes in the principal's presence. The task may be no more than to deliver a document, or orally communicate the principal's decision, when delivery or communication, as the case may be, is likely to change the principal's legal position. Such a person may be called a nuntius, or messenger. The term is not, however, one of art, and there are various other cognates, such as amanuensis, functionary, ministerial agent, and conduit,[315] depending on the task. So, an amanuensis may be asked to sign a document for the principal, who perhaps because of physical disability may not be able to sign personally.[316] Another context is the courtroom, where a barrister in some circumstances may be no more than the mouthpiece of the client, having taken specific instructions from the client, perhaps at the request of the tribunal in order immediately to convey the answer to the tribunal.[317] It may be argued that a person while performing such tasks is not an agent at all, not least because in the absence of discretion there will be limited place for the application of fiduciary duties.[318] Nonetheless, the participation of the nuntius or other ministerial agent may have been critical in effecting a change in the principal's legal position, one of the key features of agency. The issue whether or not a nuntius is an agent is likely to be significant only for a rule of law that requires personal action; the conclusion being that the proscription of delegation does not necessarily prohibit the use of a nuntius. In such cases, the relevant act is treated as effected by, as opposed to on behalf of, the principal. Such a rule is more likely to be statutory,[319] or created by a contract, since the normal position of the common law is that whatever can be done personally can be done by an agent.[320] But the rule, for example, that requires a deed to be executed by the party making the deed (unless an attorney is authorised by a separate deed to do so) can be met by the use of an amanuensis, with the principal present.[321] More broadly, the lack of discretion that most ministerial agents possess will register in the operation of the general principles of agency law. The mere fact, for example, that a delivery agent regularly delivers documents for a principal might well lead a third party to assume a document so delivered is genuine, but would not allow that party to pass the risk of forgery to the principal.[321a] Similarly, the knowledge of a ministerial agent relevant to a legal issue is less likely to be imputed to a principal than that of an agent who has a central role in the making of a transaction.[321b]

[315] See below, para.9-129 (ministerial agents not liable for conversion).

[316] See, e.g. *Barrett v Bem* [2012] EWCA Civ 52; [2012] Ch. 573 (signing will by direction of testator); *Ramsay v Love* [2015] EWHC 65 (Ch) at [7] (operation of signature machine by another); *Cameron v Cameron* [2021] EWHC 229 (Ch) at [155] (insufficient evidence of approval by principal).

[317] See the oblique reference to this idea in *Dunhill v Burgin* [2014] UKSC 18; [2014] 1 W.L.R. 933 at [31].

[318] See, e.g. *Torre Asset Funding Ltd v The Royal Bank of Scotland Plc* [2013] EWHC 2670 (Ch) at [30] (limited agency of lead bank for syndicated lenders, but more than mere postal service); *Marme Inversiones 2007 SL v Natwest Markets Plc* [2019] EWHC 366 (Comm) at [444] (lead arranging bank not acting as agent in setting terms of financing). See further below, para.6-037.

[319] See, e.g. *Hilmi & Associates Ltd v 20 Pembridge Villas Freehold Ltd* [2010] EWCA Civ 314; [2010] 1 W.L.R. 2750 (Leasehold Reform Housing and Urban Development Act 1993), and fn.187, above.

[320] See below, para.2-017. See too para.2-023.

[321] See below, Article 10.

[321a] See, e.g. *Spooner v Browning* [1898] 1 Q.B. 528, Article 75, Illustration 1.

[321b] For discussion, see below, paras.8-211 and 8-212.

CREATION OF AGENCY

1. GENERAL

COMMENT

Apparent authority and estoppel

Replace footnote 10 with:

[10] See *Premium Nafta Products Ltd v Fili Shipping Co Ltd* [2007] UKHL 40; [2008] 1 Lloyd's Rep. 254 **2-005**
(arbitration clause); and *Deutsche Bank AG v Asia Pacific Broadband Wireless Communications Inc*

[2008] EWCA Civ 1091; [2008] 2 Lloyd's Rep. 619 at [25] (jurisdiction clause). See further below, para.3-013.

COMMENT

Rule (3) Agent acting for both parties to a transaction

Replace paragraph with:

2-015   The agent of one party is not incompetent to act as agent of the other. Thus solicitors frequently act for both the buyer and the seller of a house or for both lender and borrower. Whether an agent has in fact acted for more than one party is always a question of fact. The mere preparation of documents for the counterparty of a principal to sign, such as a form of minutes, would not make the drafter the agent of the counterparty.[75a] Nor does the fact that the counterparty pays the agent's remuneration necessarily result in the agent acting for both sides.[75b] While an agent is competent to act for both sides, there are many judicial warnings as to the dangers of this practice.[76] It is perhaps more likely that an agent can acceptably acquire the second capacity after the relevant contract has been made.[77] Although there may not be an implied term of the traditional sort in the contract of agency that would preclude the agent's acting for the other party,[78] the rules of equity will apply to the situation, and equity presumes that a person in a fiduciary position must avoid conflicts of interest unless the parties assent to the conflict.[79] Equity may intervene with an injunction in appropriate cases.[80] Otherwise, agents who act for both parties run grave risks of finding themselves in a position in which their duty to one party is inconsistent with their duty to the other, for example as regards information coming into their possession. In such a case the agent will be in breach of the agent's duty to the first principal, and liable accordingly, unless that principal has given informed consent to the transaction with the other principal.[81] Where the agent's acts result in a transaction with a third party who knew of the agent's dual capacity, that transaction may be voidable.[82] But in other cases an action taken by the agent on behalf of the other principal may be valid in itself, though wrongful.[83] In a slightly different context, the employee of one party can in principle be agent for another.[84]

[75a] *NDH Properties Ltd v Lupton Fawcett LLP* [2020] EWHC 3056 (Ch) at [97].

[75b] See *Plevin v Paragon Personal Finance Ltd* [2014] UKSC 61; [2014] 1 W.L.R. 4222 at [33]; and para.1-004, above.

[76] See *Moody v Cox and Hatt* [1917] 2 Ch. 71 at 91; *Spector v Ageda* [1973] Ch. 30 at 47; below, para.6-048. For other examples of agents acting for both parties see *Emmerson v Heelis* (1809) 2 Taunt. 38 (auctioneer); *Newsholme v Road Transport Insurance Co*, Illustration 2 to Article 95 (insurance agent); *Briess v Woolley* [1954] A.C. 333 (director); *The Giancarlo Zeta* [1966] 2 Lloyd's Rep. 317 (freight broker) (Can.); *BS Developments No.12 Ltd v PB & SF Properties Ltd* (2006) 7 N.Z. Conveyancing and Property R. 603 (real estate agent found to act for both sides); *Halloran v Minister Administering National Parks and Wildlife Act 1974* [2006] HCA 3; (2006) 229 C.L.R. 545 at [56] (director acts for two companies simultaneously); *Newcastle United Plc v Revenue and Customs Commissioners* [2007] EWHC 612 (Ch); [2007] S.T.C. 1330 (sports agent acting for two parties). For further discussion, see below, para.2-033.

[77] See Story, *Agency* (1839), § 31; and *Royal Securities Corp Ltd v Montreal Trust Co* (1966) 59 D.L.R. (2d) 666; affirmed (1967) 63 D.L.R. (2d) 15; *P&P Property Ltd v Owen White and Catlin LLP* [2018] EWCA Civ 1082 (solicitor for vendor limited agent for solicitor for purchaser under Law Society's Code for Completion by Post).

[78] *Newcastle United Plc v Revenue and Customs Commissioners* [2007] EWHC 612 (Ch); [2007] S.T.C. 1330 at [29].

[79] See below, Article 44, and in particular para.6-048. See too *UBS AG (London Branch) v Kommunale Wasserwerke Peipkiz GmbH* [2017] EWCA Civ 1567 at [95] (conflict of interest a pointer away from dual agency).

[80] See below, para.6-044.

[81] *Fullwood v Hurley* [1928] 1 K.B. 498 at 502; *Anglo-African Merchants Ltd v Bayley* [1970] 1 Q.B. 311 (insurance broker); *Eagle Star Insurance Co Ltd v Spratt* [1971] 2 Lloyd's Rep. 116 at 133; *Richard Ellis Ltd v Van Hong-tuan* [1988] 1 H.K.L.R. 169; *Hilton v Barker Booth and Eastwood* [2005] UKHL 8; [2005] 1 W.L.R. 567. See further below, para.6-039.

[82] *Re a Debtor* [1927] 2 Ch. 367; *Taylor v Walker* [1958] 1 Lloyd's Rep. 490; *North and South Trust Co v Berkeley* [1971] 1 W.L.R. 470 at 485. See further Article 96.

[83] See Illustration 3.

[84] *Man Nutzfahrzeuge AG v Ernst & Young* [2005] EWHC (Comm) 2347 at [99], per Moore-Bick J; though in general not at the same time and in relation to the same transaction; affirmed on other points [2007] EWCA Civ 910.

COMMENT

Form of signature

Replace paragraph with:

The reference above to signature "in his name" can be taken to suggest that the agent should write the principal's name first, adding, optionally, the agent's own signature below, and there is further support for such a requirement in the case cited:

2-023

> "On this view if Richard Roe wished to sign as agent for John Doe he can sign John Doe by his agent Richard Roe, but he cannot sign Richard Roe as agent for John Doe."[136]

This would be the rule unless there was an indication in the relevant wording that the agent could sign in the agent's name first, indicating if desired the person for whom the agent had signed. The latter procedure is justified, for example, in the case of the Statute of Frauds, which contemplated signature by an agent "thereunto lawfully authorised"[137] and by the Powers of Attorney Act 1971,[138] which refers in s.7 to signature and other acts by the agent "in his own name". However, despite the above dicta, the inflexibility of such reasoning (the burden of which would be quite unknown to most signers who had not taken legal advice and to many who had) makes the approach doubtful: it has been said in the Australian decisions[139] that such requisites for ordinary signature by an agent should not be rigidly insisted on, at least unless the wording of the enabling provision appears to require it.[140] The crucial question must surely be whether signature by an agent is permissible: so long as the purport of such a signature is clear, it is difficult to see that the form should be of particular consequence.[140a] It seems also that an electronic signature may suffice for the purposes of the Statute of Frauds and its amending Acts.[141] It is not yet clear whether a footer with the sender's name and contact details automatically generated at the end of an email would be sufficient, particularly where it was evident from previous correspondence that the sender normally typed his or her name above the footer; it is well known that accidents can happen in the use of computerised communications.[142]

[136] *McRae v Coulton* (1989) 7 N.S.W.L.R. 644 at 664, per Hope JA. See also *UBAF Ltd v European American Banking Corp* [1982] Q.B. 713; Article 91.

[137] *Graham v Musson* (1839) 5 Bing. N.C. 603.

[138] As amended by Law of Property (Miscellaneous Provisions) Act 1989 Schs 1 and 2.

[139] See *McRae v Coulton* (1989) 7 N.S.W.L.R. 644, at 666; *Nielsen v Capital Finance Australia Ltd* [2014] QCA 139.

[140] See 664. An example is s.91 of the Bills of Exchange Act 1882, which provides that it is "sufficient if his signature is written thereon by some other person or under his authority".

140a See, e.g. *Prempeh v Lakhany* [2020] EWCA Civ 1422.

141 *Lindsay v O'Loughnane* [2010] EWHC 529 (QB); [2012] B.C.C. 153 at [95]; *Golden Ocean Group Ltd v Salgaocar Mining Industries PVT Ltd* [2012] EWCA Civ 265; [2012] 1 W.L.R. 3674 at [32]; affg [2011] EWHC 56 (Comm); [2011] 1 W.L.R. 2575 at [95]; *WS Tankship II BV v The Kwangju Bank Ltd* [2011] EWHC 3103 (Comm) at [155]; *Ramsay v Love* [2015] EWHC 65 (Ch) at [7].

142 cf. *Neocleous v Rees* [2019] EWHC 2462 (Ch) (where the words "many thanks" had been typed above the footer).

3. RATIFICATION

COMMENT

In existence when act done

Replace paragraph with:

2-064   The requirement that the principal exist at the time of the alleged contract arises most commonly in relation to contracts made on behalf of companies not yet registered.[383] Where the promoters of a prospective company enter into a contract on its behalf before its incorporation, the company cannot after incorporation ratify the contract, because it was not in existence at the time when the contract was made and so could not have made the contract at that time.[384] The company may make a new contract on the same terms as the old,[385] and this may be proved by part performance,[386] but it cannot ratify the contract with retrospective effect. Other remedies have sometimes been found in respect of pre-incorporation contracts[387]; but it has also been held that a company is not bound in equity to pay for work done before its formation, even though it has taken the benefit of the work.[388] Such results have proved inconvenient in practice and in some jurisdictions are changed by statute.[389] Issues relating to the existence of the principal also arise with unidentified principals and are discussed below.[390]

383 See Companies Act 2006 s.16.

384 *Kelner v Baxter* (1866–67) L.R. 2 C.P. 174, Illustration 6; *Re Empress Engineering Co* (1880–81) 16 Ch.D. 125; *Re Northumberland Avenue Hotel Co* (1886) 33 Ch.D. 16; *Melhado v Porto Alegre, etc., Ry Co* (1873–74) L.R. 9 C.P. 503; *Natal Land, etc., Co v Pauline, etc., Syndicate* [1904] A.C. 120; *Gibbons v Doherty* [2020] IESC 72 at [78]. But the person acting for the company may be personally liable: see Article 107.

385 *Howard v Patent Ivory Co* (1888) 38 Ch.D. 156; cf. *Touche v Metropolitan Ry Warehousing Co* (1870–71) L.R. 6 Ch.App. 671.

386 *Howard v Patent Ivory Co* (1888) 38 Ch.D. 156; cf. *Touche v Metropolitan Ry Warehousing Co* (1870–71) L.R. 6 Ch.App. 671.

387 See *Re Empress Engineering Co* (1880–81) 16 Ch.D. 125; *Re Dale & Plant* (1889) 61 L.T. 206; *Rover International Ltd v Cannon Film Sales Ltd (No.3)* [1989] 1 W.L.R. 912; *Gower's Principles of Modern Company Law* (10th edn), paras 5-24–5-28.

388 *Re English & Colonial Produce Co* [1906] 2 Ch. 435.

389 Companies Act (Singapore) cap.50 s.41; Companies Ordinance (Hong Kong) s.32A; Corporations Act 2001 (Cth) ss.131–132; Companies Act 1993 (NZ) ss.182–185; Companies Act 2014 (Ire) s.45. See too *Rolle Family & Co Ltd v Rolle* [2017] UKPC 35; [2018] A.C. 205 As to Ireland, see *Gibbons v Doherty* [2020] IESC 72 at [92].

390 See below, para.2-067.

CHAPTER 3

AUTHORITY OF AGENTS

1. ACTUAL AND APPARENT AUTHORITY

COMMENT

Arbitration clauses and jurisdiction clauses

Replace footnote 100 with:

[100] *Premium Nafta Products Ltd v Fili Shipping Co Ltd* [2007] UKHL 40; [2007] 4 All E.R. 951; [2007] 2 All E.R. (Comm) 1053 (affirming the Court of Appeal, sub nom. *Fiona Trust and Holding Corp v Privalov* [2007] EWCA Civ 20; [2007] 2 Lloyd's Rep. 267; [2007] 1 All E.R. (Comm) 891). See also *Interprods Ltd v De La Rue International Ltd* [2014] EWHC 68 (Comm) at [7]; and *Republic of Mozambique v Credit Suisse International* [2021] EWCA Civ 329.   **3-013**

[11]

CHAPTER 5

SUB-AGENCY

Article 35

RELATION BETWEEN PRINCIPAL AND SUB-AGENT

Replace list item "(2)" with:

(2)   The relation of principal and agent may be established by an agent between   **5-008**
the principal and a sub-agent if the agent is expressly or impliedly authorised
to constitute such relation, or if the agent's act is ratified, and it is the intention of the agent and of such sub-agent that such relation should be
constituted.[44]

[44] *De Bussche v Alt* (1878) 8 Ch.D. 286, Illustration 5; *Sotheby's v Mark Weiss Ltd* [2020] EWCA Civ
1570 (co-owner enters into agency contract in one name only). Alternatively, it may be found that,
properly construed, there was no intermediate agency but a direct agency made through one of the
principal's agents: *Homecare Direct Shopping Pty Ltd v Gray* [2008] VSCA 111.

COMMENT

Apparent authority

Replace paragraph with:
This Article again deals with actual authority. But it should be remembered that   **5-015**
the principles of apparent authority still apply where third parties are involved. Thus
a person appointed as sub-agent to the principal by another agent may be able to
rely on the apparent authority of the appointing agent if there was some specific
representation by the principal, or if the case is one where authority to delegate
would normally be implied, despite instructions not to delegate given by the
principal to the agent but unknown to the appointed agent. And a person dealing
with an agent so appointed may be able to rely on the principal's holding out such
person as an agent, or on the apparent authority of the appointing agent to make the
appointment. So also a person may be able to rely on apparent authority to be appointed as a sub-agent, e.g. where the sub-agent wishes to exercise a lien. It seems
that where the agent who appoints the sub-agent has only apparent authority to
make the appointment, third parties who deal with the sub-agent (whether disclosed
or not) need not establish that they knew of the original holding out. The principal
is precluded from denying the sub-agent's actual authority to bind, so long at least

[13]

as there has been no communication otherwise, or nothing else to put the sub-agent or third party on inquiry.[107] The basis for this result seems to be the justice of the sub-agent's position. The sub-agent should be able to rely on the head-agent's apparent authority, lest the sub-agent become liable to the third party in breach of warranty of authority. The sub-agent should not have to rely on a right of indemnity from the principal. The position will be different where the sub-agent exceeds the scope of the expressly delegated authority; there it may be necessary for the third party to show that it relied on the chain of representations.[108] Where the appointment of the sub-agent is without actual authority, and there is no apparent authority, the principal will not in general be bound by the acts of such a sub-agent.[109]

[107] *AJU Remicon Co Ltd v Alida Shipping Co Ltd* [2007] EWHC 2246 (Comm) at [18]. See too *Ciban Management Corp v Citco (BVI) Ltd* [2020] UKPC 21; [2020] 3 W.L.R. 705 (noted P. Watts, "Acting on the Apparent Authority of Shareholders" (2021) 137 L.Q.R. 20).

[108] See *Ing Re (UK) Ltd v R & V Versicherung AG* [2006] EWHC 1544 (Comm); [2006] 2 All E.R. (Comm) 870; [2006] Lloyd's Rep. I.R. 653; [2007] 1 B.C.L.C. 108 at [100]; *Flexirent Capital Pty Ltd v EBS Consulting Pty Ltd* [2007] VSC 158 at [213].

[109] See *Schmaling v Tomlinson* (1815) 6 Taunt. 147; *Mason v Clifton* (1863) 3 F. & F. 899.

ILLUSTRATIONS

Replace list item "(5)" with:

5-017   (5)   A ship was consigned to A, an agent in China, for sale, a minimum price being fixed. A employed B to sell the ship in circumstances in which he had authority to do so.[124] B, being unable to find a purchaser, bought the ship himself at the minimum price, and subsequently resold it at a large profit. It was held that privity of contract existed between the principal and B, and that B was liable to account to the principal for the profit made on the resale.[125]

[124] See Article 34, Illustration 7.

[125] *De Bussche v Alt.* (1878) 8 Ch.D. 286; see also *Tarn v Scanlan* [1928] A.C. 34; *Sotheby's v Mark Weiss Ltd* [2020] EWCA Civ 1570. But see above, text to fn.83.

CHAPTER 6

DUTIES OF AGENTS TOWARDS THEIR PRINCIPALS

[15]

1.   DUTIES OF PERFORMANCE

COMMENT

Contract, tort or both?

Replace paragraph with:

6-018   A gratuitous agent's liability, if any, cannot lie in contract and must clearly lie in tort.[88] Where the agency is contractual, however, it is obvious that the primary action is one for breach of contract. Where what is alleged is negligence, as it often is, the question then arises whether it is possible to sue in tort instead of contract. There may be advantages in doing so, particularly in connection with the running of limitation periods. For in contract time runs from the moment of the breach (but the position can be different if there is an ongoing duty of performance[88a]); in tort, since the gist of the action is damage, it runs from when damage is suffered.[89] The matter has been one of dispute for a considerable time in common law jurisdictions. For England, it is clear that an action in tort may concurrently lie in some circumstances,[90] with the incidental advantages that this may bring.[91]

[88] See Article 42.

[88a] Courts will usually avoid finding a continuing duty where it is simply a device to extend limitation periods: *Maharaj v Johnson* [2015] UKPC 28; [2015] P.N.L.R. 27 at [32]–[34]; *Sciortino v Beaumont* [2021] EWCA Civ 786; [2021] 3 W.L.R. 343 at [47].

[89] Some relief is provided by Limitation Act 1980 s.2.

[90] *Henderson v Merrett Syndicates Ltd* [1995] 2 A.C. 145. See also *Midland Bank Trust Co Ltd v Hett, Stubbs & Kemp* [1979] Ch. 384, holding a solicitor liable in contract and tort, the reasoning of which was approved in the *Henderson* case; *Equitas Ltd v Walsham Brothers & Co Ltd* [2013] EWHC 3264 (Comm) at [57]; *Berney v Saul (t/a Thomas Saul & Co)* [2013] EWCA Civ 640 (limitation issues); *Maharaj v Johnson* [2015] UKPC 28 (solicitors' negligence); *Central Trust Co v Rafuse* [1986] 2 S.C.R. 147; (1986) 31 D.L.R. (4th) 481 (Canada); *Hill v van Erp* (1997) 188 C.L.R. 159 (Australia); *R.M. Turton & Co v Kerslake & Partners* [2000] 3 N.Z.L.R. 406 (New Zealand); *Wellesley Partners LLP v Withers LLP* [2015] EWCA Civ 1146; *Caliendo v Mishcon De Reya (A Firm)* [2016] EWHC 150 (Ch) (solicitor assumed limited duties of care to shareholder of client company); *Golden Belt 1 Sukuk Co BSC(c) v BNP Paribas* [2017] EWHC 3182 (Comm); [2018] Bus. L.R. 816 (duty of care owed by bank intermediary to holders of promissory notes to obtain debtor's signature). See too *Arthur JS Hall & Co v Simons* [2002] 1 A.C. 615 at 688. As to tortious liability for exceeding mandate, see above, para.6-005.

[91] As to the pleading of contributory negligence in contract cases see Treitel, *Law of Contract* (15th edn), para.20-112 onwards; *Chitty on Contracts* (33rd edn), para.26-085; *Forsikringsaktieselskapet Vesta v Butcher* [1986] 2 All E.R. 488; affirmed on other grounds [1989] A.C. 852; *Youell v Bland Welch & Co Ltd (the Superhulls Cover case) (No.2)* [1990] 2 Lloyd's Rep. 431; and *Dunlop Haywards (DHL) Ltd v Barbon Insurance Group Ltd* [2009] EWHC 2900 (Comm); [2010] Lloyd's Rep I.R. 149 (not established against principal, but established by sub-agent against agent).

Information

Replace footnote 116 with:

6-021   [116] See, e.g. *National Home Loans Corp Plc v Giffen Couch & Archer* [1998] 1 W.L.R. 207 (default on existing mortgage not reported to client lender but existing credit performance of debtor not within instructions); *Torre Asset Funding Ltd v The Royal Bank of Scotland Plc* [2013] EWHC 2670 (Ch) at [156] (agent in syndicated lending had assumed limited duties, and was not required to assess whether an event of default by a borrower had occurred in order to inform principals); *Bishopsgate Contracting Solutions Ltd v O'Sullivan* [2021] EWHC 2103 (QB) at [221].

Illegal conduct

Replace footnote 121 with:

[121] cf. *Re Vining Sparks Ltd* [2019] EWHC 2885 (Ch); [2020] S.T.C. 410 (tax avoidance by director on legal advice). See too *Lennon v Englefield* [2021] EWHC 1473 (QB) (loss not caused by failure to comply with Money Laundering Regulations 2007).

6-023

2. FIDUCIARY AND OTHER EQUITABLE DUTIES

COMMENT

Agent as fiduciary

Replace the fourth paragraph with:

Even where the relationship is contractual (as it normally will be), the relevance of the contract will usually be only to modify duties that would otherwise be implied by equity. Rarely, however, a contract may contain an express clause prohibiting a conflict of interest.[218a] Otherwise, the vulnerability of the principal has for more than two centuries[219] been recognised as requiring a degree of supervision. The relief is principally given by the application of fiduciary duties, though other equitable (or partly equitable) doctrines such as duress or undue influence and the special rules for confidential information may on occasion be relevant. The agreement of the parties or the background of the case may however establish that the relationship is not one of agency[220] or that a fiduciary relationship either did not exist or had been modified from the normal standards[221]; but equally a fiduciary relationship may, while consistent with them, increase the contract duties.[222] The long-standing application of fiduciary duties to company promoters, who may have had no appointment, contractual or otherwise, with the claimant company, and who sometimes show little conscious regard for the interests of investors, is an example of the reach of equitable doctrine.[223] Similar considerations apply to those, admittedly circumscribed, cases where company directors have been found to have assumed a responsibility to advise shareholders.[224]

6-035

[218a] See *Secretariat Consulting Pte Ltd v A Company* [2021] EWCA Civ 6; [2021] 4 W.L.R. 20 at [71] (expert witnesses).

[219] See *York Buildings v MacKenzie* (1795) 8 Bro. P.C. 42. See further, Getzler, in *Philosophical Foundations of Fiduciary Law* (Gold and Miller eds, 2014), Ch.2.

[220] See *Coachcraft Ltd v SVP Fruit Co Ltd* (1980) 28 A.L.R. 319 at 328–329 (PC) (proxy with no obligations to vote as shareholder directed).

[221] See *Hospital Products Ltd v US Surgical Corp* (1984) 156 C.L.R. 41 at 96–97, per Mason J. See para.1-020, and para.6-056.

[222] See Mason J in the *Hospital Products* (1984) 156 C.L.R. 41 case, at 99; *Conway v Ratiu* [2005] EWCA Civ 1302; [2006] 1 All E.R. 571 at [74]; *Cia. Fianciera "Soleada" SA v Hamoor Tanker Corp Inc (The Borag)* [1980] 1 Lloyd's Rep. 111 (reversed on a different point [1981] 1 W.L.R. 274) (unusual terms imposed higher duty of loyalty); *John Youngs Insurance Services Ltd v Aviva Insurance Service UK Ltd* [2011] EWHC 1515 (TCC) at [120] (duty to account survives termination of contract).

[223] See *Erlanger v New Sombrero Phosphate Co* (1878) 3 App.Cas. 1218; *Gluckstein v Barnes* [1900] A.C. 240. See also *Bagnall v Carlton* (1877) 6 Ch.D. 371; *Emma Silver Mining Co v Lewis & Sons* (1879) 4 C.P.D. 396; *Emma Silver Mining Co v Grant* (1879) 11 Ch.D. 918; *Whaley Bridge Calico Printing Co v Green* (1879) 5 Q.B.D. 109; *Lydney and Wigpool Ore Co v Bird* (1886) 33 Ch.D. 85; *Re Cape Breton Co* (1885) 29 Ch.D. 795; affirmed sub nom. *Cavendish-Bentinck v Fenn* (1887) 12 App.Cas. 652; *Lagunas Nitrate Co v Lagunas Syndicate* [1899] 2 Ch. 392; *Re Lady Forrest (Murchison) Gold Mine* [1901] 1 Ch. 582; *Re Leeds & Hanley Theatres of Varieties* [1902] 2 Ch. 809; *Omnium Electric Palaces Ltd v Baines* [1914] 1 Ch. 332; *Jacobus Marler Estates Ltd v Marler* (1916) 85 L.J.P.C. 167n.; *Jubilee Cotton Mills v Lewis* [1924] A.C. 958; *Tracy v Mandelay Pty Ltd* (1953) 88 C.L.R. 215.

224 *Briess v Woolley* [1954] A.C. 333; *Coleman v Myers* [1977] 2 N.Z.L.R. 225; *Brunninghausen v Glavanics* (1999) 46 N.S.W.L.R. 538 (noted by Goddard (2000) 116 L.Q.R. 197); *Park's of Hamilton (Holdings) Ltd v Campbell* [2014] CSIH 36; 2014 SC 726 at [27]; *Kiriwai Consultants Ltd v Holmes* [2015] NZCA 149. cf. *Percival v Wright* [1902] 2 Ch. 421.

Are all agents always fiduciaries?

Replace footnote 233 with:

6-037   233 See *Meagher, Gummow and Lehane's Equity Doctrines and Remedies* (5th edn), para.5-210 onwards; R. Flannigan, "Fiduciary Agency Denied" [2021] J.B.L. 50.

Replace footnote 235 with:

235 *Coachcraft Ltd v SVP Fruit Co Ltd* (1980) 28 A.L.R. 319 at 328–329 (PC) (proxy but with no obligations to vote as shareholder directed). See too *UBS AG (London Branch) v Kommunale Wasserwerke Leipzig GmbH* [2017] EWCA Civ 1567 at [92].

When do fiduciary duties start and end?

Replace footnote 253 with:

6-038   253 See *Medsted Associates Ltd v Canaccord Genuity Wealth (International) Ltd* [2019] EWCA Civ 83; [2019] 1 W.L.R. 4481 at [32] and [44]; *Rahme v Benjamin & Khoury Pty Ltd* [2019] NWSCA 211. See too *Belsner v Cam Legal Services Ltd* [2020] EWHC 2755 (QB).

Disclosure and consent

Replace footnote 272 with:

6-039   272 See *Keppel v Wheeler* [1927] 1 K.B. 577, Illustration 6 to Article 60; and *Pengelly v Business Mortgage Finance 4 Plc* [2020] EWHC 2002 (Ch) at [68] (affd *Wood v Commercial First Business Ltd* [2021] EWCA Civ 471; [2021] 3 W.L.R. 395 on other points).

Replace footnote 278 with:

278 *Cook v Deeks* [1916] 1 A.C. 554. As to consent from a liquidator in the form of sale of company assets to a director, see *Brown v Bennett* [1999] 1 B.C.L.C. 649; and *Courtwood Holdings SA v Woodley Properties Ltd* [2018] EWHC 2163 (Ch). Despite these decisions, it is doubtful whether a liquidator's consent should bind shareholders inter se where the shareholders were in a quasi-partnership and owed one another fiduciary duties (one of the parties may have induced the company's liquidation).

Remedies: agent holding money for principal

Replace footnote 299 with:

6-041   299 See *New Zealand and Australian Land Co v Watson* (1881) 7 Q.B.D. 374 at 382; *Templeton Insurance Ltd v Motorcare Warranties Ltd* [2010] EWHC 3113 (Comm) at [194]; *Bieber v Teathers Ltd* [2012] EWHC 190 (Ch) at [25]; affirmed [2012] EWCA Civ 1466; [2012] 2 B.C.L.C. 585 (no trust where impossible to carry out instructions if keep moneys separate); *National Stadium Project (Grenada) Corp v NH International (Caribbean) Ltd* [2020] UKPC 25 at [38].

Remedies: profits made in breach of duty to principal

Replace footnote 309 with:

6-042   309 The detail as to how an account of profits is measured is beyond the scope of this book. For discussion, see P. Devonshire, *Account of Profits* (2013); M. Conaglen, "Identifying the Profits for which a Fiduciary Must Account" [2020] C.L.J. 38. See too *Gray v Global Energy Horizons Corp* [2020] EWCA Civ 1668; [2021] 1 W.L.R. 2264.

Replace footnote 320 with:

320 Support for the view that a company director can be accountable for gains made by third parties as a result of the director's breach of duty can be found in *CMS Dolphin Ltd v Simonet* [2001] 2 B.C.L.C. 704. See too *Walsham v Stainton* (1863) 1 De G.J. & S. 678. But cf. *Ultraframe (UK) Ltd v Fielding* [2005] EWHC 1638 (Ch) at [1575]–[1576]; *Fiona Trust Holding Corp v Privalov* [2007] EWHC 1217 (Comm) at [29]; *National Grid Electricity Transmission Plc v McKenzie Harbour Management*

Resources Ltd [2009] EWHC 1817 (Ch) at [118] (indicating special rules where the defaulting agent is a member of a partnership which derives the resulting gains); *Aerostar Maintenance International Ltd v Wilson* [2010] EWHC 2032 (Ch) at [204]; *Novoship (UK) Ltd v Mikhaylyuk* [2012] EWHC 3586 (Comm) at [99] (issue not addressed on appeal: [2014] EWCA Civ 908; [2015] Q.B. 499); *Lifestyle Equities CV v Ahmed* [2021] EWCA Civ 675; [2021] Bus. L.R. 1020 at [17]. See too *Northampton Regional Livestock Centre Co Ltd v Cowling* [2015] EWCA Civ 651; [2016] 1 B.C.L.C. 431 at [96] (partner liable for improper profit derived by colleague in the course of partnership).

Losses caused: equitable restitution and compensation

Replace footnote 349 with:

[349] See *Swindle v Harrison* [1997] 4 All E.R. 705, Illustration 12; *Nationwide BS v Balmer Radmore* [1999] Lloyd's Rep. P.N. 241; *Collins v Brebner* [2000] Lloyd's Rep. P.N. 587. But cf. *Bristol & West BS v May, May & Merrimans* [1996] 2 All E.R. 801, where there were positive misrepresentations by the fiduciary. See also *Gilbert v Shanahan* [1998] 3 N.Z.L.R. 528; *Mantonella Pty Ltd v Thompson* (2009) 255 A.L.R. 367; *Rawleigh v Tait* [2008] NZCA 525; [2009] N.Z. Family L.R. 802; *Break Fast Investments Pty Ltd v Rigby Cooke Lawyers (A Firm)* [2021] VSC 398 at [267]. For discussion of *Swindle* and later cases, see Conaglen (2010) 126 L.Q.R. 72 at 81–86.

6-043

Other remedies: rescission, injunction, and declaration

Replace footnote 358 with:

[358] e.g. *Maguire v Makaronis* (1997) 188 C.L.R. 449. For more detailed discussion, see Article 45 and para.6-068 in particular. In respect of company directors, see Companies Act 2006 s.178(1).

6-044

COMMENT

Conflict of duty and duty

Replace the first paragraph with:

One manifestation of the agent's fiduciary duty to avoid conflicts is that the agent must not serve two principals whose interests may conflict. In principle, conflicts of duty and duty attract the same consequences as conflicts of duty and interest.[388a] So agents may not act for both parties to a transaction unless they ensure that they fully disclose all the material facts to each party and obtain their informed consent to their so acting.[389] In this situation there is not preferment of the agent's own interest, but equally the agent may not act entirely in the interests of either single principal. There may also be breach of the duty of loyalty in the sense that the loyalty must be undivided.[390] In such cases the agent may cause loss to one by failure to disclose information acquired in connection with the other—information, indeed, the disclosure of which would be a breach of duty to the first.[391]

6-048

[388a] See *Break Fast Investments Pty Ltd v Rigby Cooke Lawyers (A Firm)* [2021] VSC 398 at [119].

[389] This passage was cited with approval by Megaw J in *Anglo-African Merchants Ltd v Bayley* [1970] 1 Q.B. 311 at 323; and by Douglas J in *Dargusch v Sherley Investments Pty Ltd* [1970] Qd.R. 338 at 347; see also *Eagle Star Insurance Co Ltd v Spratt* [1971] 2 Lloyd's Rep. 116 at 133; *McDonnell v Barton Realty Ltd* [1992] 3 N.Z.L.R. 418. cf. *Swain v Law Society* [1983] 1 A.C. 598 (statutory scheme for solicitors' insurance).

[390] *Beach Petroleum NL v Kennedy* (1999) 48 N.S.W.L.R. 1. See *Snell's Equity* (34th edn), para.7-036.

[391] See also *Bristol and West BS v Mothew* [1998] Ch. 1 at 18–20.

After the second paragraph, add new paragraph:

Notwithstanding the foregoing general principles, it is relatively common for parties with potentially conflicting interests expressly to consent to using a common agent. Where this occurs there remains an overlay of equitable principle, central aspects of which are discussed in paras 6-039 and 6-056. It is worth emphasising here that the starting assumption is that both principals will expect the common agent not to be inhibited from advancing their respective interests concurrently, as if acting for only one of them.[397a] Where the parties have expressly agreed, or the context of their relationships otherwise requires, that the agent can act in a way that is not absolutely even-handed, it will still not be inferred that the agent is permitted to act in a way that is positively inimical to the interests of one principal.[397b]

[397a] See *Bristol and West Building Society v Mothew* [1998] Ch. 1 at 19.

[397b] See *Bristol and West Building Society v Mothew* [1998] Ch. 1 at 19.

Fourth paragraph, after "interests, would be", replace "acceptable." with:
inferred by a court.

Situation 1: "same matter" conflicts

Replace footnote 414 with:

6-050   [414] See *Secretariat Consulting Pte Ltd v A Company* [2021] EWCA Civ 6; [2021] 4 W.L.R. 20 (expert in litigation placing itself in position of conflict, but held not a fiduciary).

Statutory requirements

Replace paragraph with:

6-055   Sometimes disclosure of a conflict is required by statute or statutory instrument. Most obviously, the Companies Act 2006 contains rules for dealing with the conflicts of interest of company directors.[447a] Persons engaged in estate agency work are in some circumstances required to disclose to their clients services which they or persons connected with them offer to purchasers[448]; or that they or persons connected with them are seeking to acquire an interest in the land concerned.[449] Statutory requirements would usually be taken as supplemental to, rather than a replacement for, equity's requirements unless the statute were clear on the point.[450]

[447a] Companies Act 2006 s.177. For discussion of the section, albeit in a case involving predecessor provisions, see *Fairford Water Ski Club Ltd v Cohoon* [2021] EWCA Civ 143.

[448] Estate Agents (Undesirable Practices) (No.2) Order 1991 (SI 1991/1032) (made under Estate Agents Act 1979 s.18) reg.2; see Murdoch, *The Estate Agents and Property Misdescriptions Acts* (3rd edn), Ch.3A; *Law of Estate Agency* (5th edn), p.290 onwards. The civil remedy is that the contract may be unenforceable: Estate Agents Act 1979 s.18(5).

[449] Estate Agents (Undesirable Practices) (No.2) Order 1991 (SI 1991/1032) Sch.1 para.2; see Murdoch, above, pp.212–213.

[450] See *Barfoot & Thompson Ltd v Real Estate Agents Authority* [2016] NZCA 105. But in relation to company directors, see Companies Act 2006 s.170(3).

Modification of duties by contract: common law

Replace the second paragraph with:

6-056   Otherwise, contract terms can purport in some way to exclude or restrict the fiduciary duties which might otherwise arise. It is plain that a fiduciary could not exclude liability for personal fraud (including fraudulent non-disclosure) or deliberate breach of contract[453] though a fiduciary might, if the wording was clear enough, exclude liability for the fraud of an agent.[454] Furthermore, in the absence of the clearest language, it is unlikely that a court would find that a clause permitting a conflict was intended to permit the agent actively to prefer one party over the other, as opposed to attempting to act even-handedly. In *Bristol and West BS v Mothew* Millett LJ referred to what he called the "no inhibition principle",[455] that requires an agent acting with consent for both parties to refrain from putting himself in a position where the agent feels inhibited about doing his best for both parties. Liability for damages might ensue where this principle is not adhered to,[456] and almost certainly will where the fiduciary actively promotes the interests of one party over the other. In the latter situation the agent will have what is called an "actual conflict".

[453] *S. Pearson & Son Ltd v Dublin Corp* [1907] A.C. 351 at 355 and 362; Treitel, *Law of Contract* (15th edn), para.7-034–7-035.

[454] *HIH Casualty and General Insurance Ltd v Chase Manhattan Bank* [2003] UKHL 6; [2003] 1 All E.R. (Comm) 349, requiring express reference to fraud or very similar wording. But see the Hon. Justice K.R. Handley (2003) 119 L.Q.R. 537.

[455] *Bristol and West BS v Mothew* [1998] Ch. 1 at 19; *Consolidated Finance Ltd v Collins* [2013] EWCA Civ 475 at [59]; *Northampton Regional Livestock Centre Co Ltd v Cowling* [2015] EWCA Civ 651; [2016] 1 B.C.L.C. 431 at [77]. For discussion, see Conaglen (2009) 125 L.Q.R. 111 at 127–140.

[456] *Leeds and Holbeck Building Society v Arthur and Cole* [2002] P.N.L.R. 78; *Nationwide Building Society v Goodwin Harte* [1999] Lloyd's Rep. P.N. 338 at 345; *Barrowfen Properties Ltd v Patel* [2021] EWHC 2055 (Ch) at [549] (solicitor continuing to act for both borrower and lender once enforcement of loan is at issue).

COMMENT

Remedies of principal

Replace the first paragraph with:

A number of remedies can arise out of self-dealing and fair-dealing. While most of the relevant case law is at equity, in some cases of self-dealing, at least, the transaction will be unauthorised and treated both at law and equity as a nullity.[520] As to equity, a principal who finds, for instance, that an agent has purported to borrow the principal's money without consent may disown the loan, and either seek an account of the money or treat any asset bought with the money as belonging to the principal.[521] Otherwise, the principal may, in general, rescind any contract affected by the self-dealing and fair-dealing rules.[522] Rescission in equity is, however, a discretionary remedy, it seems, and a court may withhold it, including on the ground that the principal is not fully disowning the transaction.[523] Nonetheless, while the normal rule is that rescission is ab initio, that is a shorthand notion that should not be taken too literally, at least at equity.[524] So, it normally does not matter that the contract has been executed, since equity can make monetary adjustments, nor that the property being returned has meanwhile decreased in value.[525] However, the intervention of third party interests can preclude rescission.[526] The principal must also take proceedings within a reasonable time after discovering the truth about the transaction or may be taken to have acquiesced or affirmed.[527] Otherwise, the principal can elect to affirm,[528] but where there is doubt, the onus is on the agent to show that the principal has affirmed.[529] The principal will also usually be able to claim the profit any agent has made, for it is deemed to have been made on the principal's behalf.[530] Recent authority further suggests that the principal might, where there is a sale at an undervalue, treat the agent (and affected third parties) as holding the asset on constructive trust for the principal in proportion that the price paid by the agent bears to the true value of the asset purchased.[531] The resulting remedy might be proprietary or personal. Alternatively, if the complaint is of loss the principal may claim damages for breach of contract, or conceivably equitable compensation under the principle of *Nocton v Ashburton*.[532] Thus, where an agent has bought the principal's property, the principal can claim any profit on a resale[533] or the difference between the value of the property and the price the agent gave.[534]

6-068

520 See *Rothschild v Brookman* (1831) 5 Bli. (NS) 165 at 191–192 and at 282; *Salomons v Pender* (1865) 3 H. & C. 639.

521 See *Tang Ying Loi v Tang Ying Ip* [2017] HKCFA 3.

522 *Maguire v Makaronis* (1997) 188 C.L.R. 449 (mortgage set aside on terms).

523 *Johnson v EBS Pensioner Trustees Ltd* [2002] EWCA Civ 164; [2002] Lloyd's Rep P.N. 309; *Hurstanger Ltd v Wilson* [2007] EWCA Civ 299; [2007] 1 W.L.R. 2351; [2007] 4 All E.R. 1118 at [50]; *Fenwick v Naera* [2015] NZSC 68; [2016] 1 N.Z.L.R. 354 at [122]; *Gamatronic (UK) Ltd v Hamilton* [2016] EWHC 2225 (QB) at [218]; *Pengelly v Business Mortgage Finance 4 Plc* [2020] EWHC 2002 (Ch) (affd *Wood v Commercial First Business Ltd* [2021] EWCA Civ 471; [2021] 3 W.L.R. 395 on other points). For more detailed treatment of the remedy, see D. O'Sullivan, S. Elliott and R. Zakrzewski, *Law of Rescission* (2nd ed, 2014).

524 "The words [i.e. rescission ab initio] are sufficient for most purposes, but they should not be taken literally. Neither rescission by a party nor a judge's say so can turn the clock back to have that literal effect, and a contract avoided ab initio is not, in Newspeak, an uncontract": *FAI General Insurance Co Ltd v Ocean Marine Mutual Protection and Indemnity Association* (1997) 41 N.S.W.L.R. 559, per Giles CJ; cited with approval in *Brit Syndicates Ltd v Italaudit SPA* [2006] EWHC 341 (Comm) at [24]. See too *MacKenzie v Royal Bank of Canada* [1934] A.C. 468 PC (guarantee set aside despite lender's reliance by making loan).

525 *Armstrong v Jackson* [1917] 2 K.B. 822.

526 For sub-purchases pendente lite, see *Trevelyan v White* (1839) 1 Beav. 588.

527 *De Montmorency v Devereux* (1840) 7 C. & F. 188; *Champion v Rigby* (1830) 1 Russ. & M. 539; affirmed (1840) 9 L.J.(O.S.) Ch. 211; *Flint v Woodin* (1852) 9 Hare 618; *Lyddon v Moss* (1859) 4 De G. & J. 104; *Clanricarde v Henning* (1861) 30 Beav. 175; *Wentworth v Lloyd* (1863) 32 Beav. 467.

528 *Bentley v Craven* (1853) 18 Beav. 75; *Rea v Bell* (1852) 18 L.T.(O.S.) 312; *Gray v New Augarita Porcupine Mines* [1952] 3 D.L.R. 1 (PC); *Hely-Hutchinson v Brayhead Ltd* [1968] 1 Q.B. 549; *Robinson v Randfontein* [1921] App.D. 168 at 178.

529 *Cavendish-Bentinck v Fenn* (1887) 12 App.Cas. 652 at 666, Illustration 15. The principal must know the full facts, including the fact that he could rescind the transaction if he so wished: *Crowe v Ballard* (1790) 2 Cox Eq.Cas. 253; *Osry v Hirsch* [1922] Cape P.D. 531; *Holder v Holder* [1968] Ch. 353; *Peyman v Lanjani* [1985] Ch. 457.

530 For an example of calculation see *Estate Realties Ltd v Wignall (No.2)* [1992] 2 N.Z.L.R. 615; Watts [1992] L.M.C.L.Q. 439.

531 *Akita Holdings Ltd v Attorney General of Turks and Caicos Islands Is* [2017] UKPC 7; [2017] A.C. 590 (noted Glister (2017) 11 J.Eq. 219; P.G. Turner, "Accountability for profits derived from involvement in breach of fiduciary duty" [2018] C.L.J. 255).

532 *Nocton v Ashburton* [1914] A.C. 932; *Brickenden v London Loan & Savings Co* [1934] 3 D.L.R. 465 PC; above para.6-042. See Conaglen (2003) 119 L.Q.R. 246.

533 *Barker v Harrison* (1846) 2 Coll. 546; *De Bussche v Alt* (1878) 8 Ch.D. 286; *Blackham v Haythorpe* (1917) 23 C.L.R. 156; *Headway Construction Co Ltd v Downham* (1974) 233 E.G. 675, Illustration 17.

534 *Hall v Hallett* (1784) 1 Cox Eq.Cas. 134.

COMMENT

Confidential information

Replace footnote 602 with:

6-077 602 *Baker v Gibbons* [1972] 1 W.L.R. 693; *Peninsular Real Estate Ltd v Harris* [1992] 2 N.Z.L.R. 216; *Whitmar Publications Ltd v Gamage* [2013] EWHC 1881 (Ch) at [58]; *Travel Counsellors Ltd v Trailfinders Ltd* [2021] EWCA Civ 38.

COMMENT

Scope of principle

Replace the fourth paragraph with:

6-080 The principle the subject of this Article is a strict one, and all profits must be accounted for even if, in acquiring them, the agent has incurred a risk of loss,[636] and the principal could not personally have made the profit, has suffered no injury or has even made a profit.[637] Nor is it usually a defence for the agent to argue that it could have made the same profits by an alternative lawful route.[637a] However, the court may make an allowance to the fiduciary for skill and expenditure in making the profit[638]; and sometimes this appears to approach a share in the profit.[639]

[636] See e.g. *Burrell v Mossop* (1888) 4 T.L.R. 270; *Williams v Stevens* (1866) L.R. 1 P.C. 352.

[637] *Parker v McKenna* (1874) L.R. 10 Ch.App. 96; *Boardman v Phipps* [1967] 2 A.C. 46, Illustration 4, a case where the principal acquired great benefit as a result of the fiduciaries' action: *Industrial Development Consultants Ltd v Cooley* [1972] 1 W.L.R. 443, Illustration 7; *Warman International Ltd v Dwyer* (1995) 182 C.L.R. 544; *Akita Holdings Ltd v Attorney General of Turks and Caicos Islands* [2017] UKPC 7; [2017] A.C. 590; *Parr v Keystone Healthcare Ltd* [2019] EWCA Civ 1246 at [18]; *Langer v McKeown* [2020] EWHC 3485 (Ch) at [296].

[637a] See *Gray v Global Energy Horizons Corp* [2020] EWCA Civ 1668; [2021] 1 W.L.R. 2264 at [128].

[638] *Boardman v Phipps* [1967] 2 A.C. 46; but cf. *Guinness Plc v Saunders* [1990] 2 A.C. 663; *Imageview Management Ltd v Jack* [2009] EWCA Civ 63; [2009] 2 All E.R. 666; *Cobbetts LLP v Hodge* [2009] EWHC 786 (Ch) at [118]. See also *Yates v Finn* (1880) 13 Ch.D. 839; *Re Jarvis* [1958] 1 W.L.R. 815; *Paul A. Davies (Australia) Pty Ltd v Davies* [1983] 1 N.S.W.L.R. 440; *Nottingham University v Fishel* [2000] I.C.R. 146. See further Watts (2009) 125 L.Q.R. 369 at 374.

[639] See *O'Sullivan v Management Agency and Music Ltd* [1985] Q.B. 428; *Re Duke of Norfolk's Settlement Trusts* [1962] Ch. 61; *Re Berkeley Applegate (Investment Consultants) Ltd* [1989] Ch. 32; *Estate Realties Ltd v Wignall* [1992] 2 N.Z.L.R. 615; *Warman International Ltd v Dwyer* (1995) 182 C.L.R. 544.

Replace the fifth paragraph with:

A claim made under the principle set out in this Article is often, of course, advanced in conjunction with a claim that the agent has used property or information belonging to the principal to acquire a benefit[640]: but the present principle is wider, since it is not confined to situations where property or information has been used. Since there is, until it is generated, no property to which the right can attach, it can be said that the standard remedy is a duty to account, which is personal[641]; but where an identifiable asset is acquired in most cases the principal will have a proprietary claim.[642] The case for a proprietary remedy is most compelling where the agent was under a positive duty to obtain the asset for the principal.[643] There is some doubt whether the action in knowing receipt is an appropriate cause of action,[643a] but the account of profits and the constructive trust should provide adequate remedies.

[640] e.g. *Boardman v Phipps* [1967] 2 A.C. 46; see Article 47.

[641] *Warman International Ltd v Dwyer* (1995) 182 C.L.R. 544 at 557; *Gray v Global Energy Horizons Corp* [2020] EWCA Civ 1668; [2021] 1 W.L.R. 2264 at [459].

[642] See *FHR European Ventures LLP v Cedar Capital Partners LLC* [2014] UKSC 45; [2015] A.C. 250.

[643] e.g. *Cook v Deeks* [1916] 1 A.C. 554; *Aerostar Maintenance International Ltd v Wilson* [2010] EWHC 2032 (Ch) at [193].

[643a] See *Brown v Bennett* [1999] 1 B.C.L.C. 649; and *Courtwood Holdings SA v Woodley Properties Ltd* [2018] EWHC 2163 (Ch). cf. *Aerostar Maintenance International Ltd v Wilson* [2010] EWHC 2032 (Ch). For discussion, see J. Glister, "Trust Property and Knowing Receipt" (2020) 34 T.L.I. 3-20.

"Business (or corporate) opportunities"

Replace footnote 648 with:

[648] e.g. *Bhullar v Bhullar* [2003] 2 B.C.L.C. 241; *Langer v McKeown* [2020] EWHC 3485 (Ch) at [263]. cf. *Wilkinson v West Coast Capital Ltd* [2005] EWHC 3009 (Ch); [2007] B.C.C. 717 at [306].   **6-081**

Second paragraph, after "the time the", replace "profit is made" with:
opportunity is exploited

To the end of the sixth paragraph, add:
For further aspects of the business opportunities rule, see para.6-080.

COMMENT

Bribes and secret commissions

Replace paragraph with:

6-085   A bribe is a type of secret profit, and a clear breach of fiduciary duty. However, the rules for bribes have special features, and the area has its own specialised group of cases. Courts generally eschew attaching rigid definitions to common law concepts, and this is true of the concept of a bribe. However, two formulations much referred to in other cases follow, the latter more apposite to the broader concept of a secret commission:

> "If a gift be made to a confidential agent with the view of inducing the agent to act in favour of the donor in relation to transactions between the donor and the agent's principal and that gift is secret as between the donor and the agent—that is to say, without the knowledge and consent of the principal—then the gift is a bribe in the view of the law" : *Hovenden & Sons v Millhoff*, per Romer LJ.[686]

> "[F]or the purpose of the civil law a bribe means a payment of a secret commission, which only means (i) that the person making the payment makes it to the agent of the other person with whom he is dealing; (ii) that he makes it to that person knowing that the person is acting as the agent of the other person with whom he is dealing; and (iii) that he fails to disclose to the other person with whom he is dealing that he has made that payment to the person whom he knows to be the other person's agent": *Industries and General Mortgage Co Ltd v Lewis*, per Slade J.[687]

Where the payment is not for a corrupt purpose, a corrupt purpose being one intended to influence the agent in the performance of the agent's tasks in favour of the payer or some other outside party, it is more appropriate to refer to the arrangement as a secret commission. But absence of corruption on the third party's part makes no difference to the agent's duty to account for an undisclosed commission.[688] It is also irrelevant that the agent has not in fact been influenced or departed from duty to the principal,[689] for the acceptance of or agreement to receive a bribe is of itself a breach of the agent's general fiduciary duty, as giving an interest contrary to the agent's duty to the principal.[690] This reasoning applies also to commissions given by way of discount on payment.[691] It is generally as problematic for the third party to promise a bribe or secret commission as to pay it, although inducement will need to be proven by the principal (actual payment supplies it own proof).[692] Agents are liable in respect of bribes and secret commissions in restitution or in tort.[693] It is now also clear that a bribe which comprises money or other property is held on trust for the principal.[694] Bribes may be offered by the third party or sought by the agent,[695] can frequently be in kind (including an offer of future employment),[696] and can be paid to relatives of, trustees for, or otherwise at the direction of, the agent.[697] It is not necessary that the bribe relate to a particular transaction, and the validity of all subsequent transactions may be affected.[698] On the other hand, not all undisclosed profiting from position would amount to a bribe or secret commission. Some gains which an agent might make will be from activities that do not relate directly to the services the agent performs for the principal and their receipt could not realistically be considered as likely to influence those services.[699] In some cases, nonetheless, the agent may be accountable in equity for incidental benefits if they were derived from the agent's fiduciary position without those benefits being considered commissions or bribes.[700] Liability also does not attach to small gifts made after the conclusion of a transaction related to services performed by the agent,[701] unless it appears that such gifts were expected when the transaction was entered into, or are intended to affect future transactions[702]; nor to discounts obtained on transactions independent of the agency relationship.[703] In yet other situations, the intermediary may not be a fiduciary at all if it is clear that the intermediary was not undertaking any obligations of loyalty to the putative principal nor otherwise exercising any powers on the principal's behalf.[704] The label "agent" is not determinative of a person's fiduciary status.

[686] *Hovenden & Sons v Millhoff* (1900) 83 L.T. 41 at 43, per Romer LJ. See too *Novoship (UK) Ltd v Mikhaylyuk* [2012] EWHC 3586 (Comm) at [106] reversed on other issues [2014] EWCA Civ 908.

[687] *Industries and General Mortgage Co Ltd v Lewis* [1949] 2 All E.R. 573 at 575. See also *Taylor v Walker* [1958] 1 Lloyd's Rep. 490, Article 96, Illustration 4; *Anangel Atlas Cia. Naviera SA v Ishikawajima-Harima Heavy Industries Co Ltd* [1990] 1 Lloyd's Rep. 167 at 171, per Leggatt J: "More succinctly it may be said that a bribe consists in a commission or other inducement which is given by the third party to an agent as such, and which is secret from the principal".

[688] See *Daraydan Holdings Ltd v Solland International Ltd* [2004] EWHC 622 (Ch); [2005] Ch. 119 at [53].

[689] *Harrington v Victoria Graving Dock Co* (1878) 3 Q.B.D. 549; *Shipway v Broadwood* [1899] 1 Q.B. 369; *Re a Debtor* [1927] 2 Ch. 367; *Daraydan Holdings Ltd v Solland International Ltd* [2004] EWHC 622 (Ch); [2005] Ch. 119 at [53]; *Donegal International Ltd v Republic of Zambia* [2007] EWHC 197 (Comm); [2007] 1 Lloyd's Rep. 397 at [275]; *Fiona Trust & Holding Corp v Privalov* [2010] EWHC 3199 (Comm) at [72]; *Otkritie International Investment Management Ltd v Urumov* [2014] EWHC 191 (Comm) at [164]; *Shagang Shipping Co Ltd v HNA Group Co Ltd* [2018] EWCA Civ 1732 at [84]; reversed on the facts [2020] UKSC 34; *HKSAR v Chu Ang* [2020] HKCFA 18 (violin teacher receives undisclosed commission when assisting pupil buy violin).

[690] *Shipway v Broadwood* [1899] 1 Q.B. 369 at 373. Statements that the recipient is conclusively presumed to have been influenced (e.g. *Hovenden v Millhoff* (1900) 83 L.T. 41; *Industries and General Mortgage Co v Lewis* [1949] 2 All E.R. 573 at 578), are therefore beside the point: the Rt Hon. Lord Millett [1993] Restitution L.Rev. 7 at 13.

[691] e.g. *Turnbull v Garden* (1869) 38 L.J.Ch. 331, Illustration 2. Sometimes such transactions can be treated as a sale by the agent to his principal: see *Kimber v Barber* (1872) L.R. 8 Ch.App. 56; Article 45.

[692] *Grant v Gold Exploration & Development Syndicate Ltd* [1900] 1 Ch. 233; though the agent can only be liable in restitution where he has received the money; *Donegal International Ltd v Republic of Zambia* [2007] EWHC 197 (Comm); [2007] 1 Lloyd's Rep. 397 at [274]–[275]; *Otkritie International Investment Management Ltd v Urumov* [2014] EWHC 191 (Comm) at [68] (corrupt purpose need not be proved).

[693] *Mahesan's case* [1979] A.C. 374 at 383.

[694] *FHR European Ventures LLP v Cedar Capital Partners LLC* [2014] UKSC 45; [2015] A.C. 250. See further para.6-087.

[695] *Novoship (UK) Ltd v Mikhaylyuk* [2012] EWHC 3586 (Comm) at [106] (issue not addressed on appeal: [2014] EWCA Civ 908).

[696] See the cases cited below, para.6-087; and *Amalgamated Industrials Ltd v Johnson & Firth Brown Ltd, The Times,* 15 April 1981 (offer of future employment); *Kings Security Systems Ltd v King* [2021] EWHC 325 (Ch).

[697] *Novoship (UK) Ltd v Mikhaylyuk* [2012] EWHC 3586 (Comm) at [107] (issue not addressed on appeal: [2014] EWCA Civ 908); *Shagang Shipping Co Ltd v HNA Group Co Ltd* [2018] EWCA Civ 1732 at [84]; reversed on the facts [2020] UKSC 34.

[698] *Novoship (UK) Ltd v Mikhaylyuk* [2012] EWHC 3586 (Comm) at [109]; affirmed [2014] EWCA Civ 908 at [54]; *Otkritie International Investment Management Ltd v Urumov* [2014] EWHC 191 (Comm) at [70].

[699] See, e.g. *Anangel Atlas Cia Naviera SA v Ishikawajima-Harima Heavy Industries Co Ltd* [1990] 1 Lloyd's Rep. 167 at 174; *Rowland v Chapman* (1901) 17 T.L.R. 669.

[700] For an example in the context of the criminal law, see *Secretary for Justice v Chan Chi Wan* [2017]

HKCFA 15. See also *Fawcett v Whitehouse* (1829) 1 Russ. & M. 132; *Turnbull v Garden* (1869) 38 L.J.Ch. 331.

[701] *The Parkdale* [1897] P. 53, Illustration 1. See also *Meadow Schama & Co v C. Mitchell & Co Ltd* (1973) 228 E.G. 1511 (sum promised after commission earned: not a bribe). See too *Donegal International Ltd v Republic of Zambia* [2007] EWHC 197 (Comm); [2007] 1 Lloyd's Rep. 397 at [277]; *Bank of Ireland v Jaffery* [2012] EWHC 1377 (Ch) at [392] (side deals but for full value and not intended as inducements).

[702] See *Fiona Trust Holding Corp v Privalov* [2010] EWHC 3199 (Comm) at [73] and [1392] ("sufficient to create a 'real possibility' of a conflict between interest and duty"); *Field v R.* [2012] 3 N.Z.L.R. 1 (MP criminally liable for having received free labour on house following assistance to immigrants in electorate). See also Article 96, Illustration 1.

[703] See *London School Board v Northcroft* (1892), *Hudson's Building and Engineering Contracts* (12th edn), para.2.235 (not carried forward to later editions).

[704] See *Eze v Conway* [2019] EWCA Civ 88. cf. *McWilliam v Norton Finance (UK) Ltd* [2015] EWCA Civ 186; [2015] 1 All E.R. (Comm) 1026 at [40].

Disclosure

Replace the first paragraph with:

6-086   Active concealment is not necessary: it is sufficient that the principal did not know of the bribe.[705] Third parties who pay a commission cannot assert that they thought the agent would disclose it; the only safe approach is for the third party directly to inform the principal of the payment.[706] Furthermore, to free the agent from liability, the disclosure must be such as to enable the principal to understand the implications of the arrangement: thus a partial disclosure may be insufficient.[707] That the principal (including an appropriate other agent of the principal[708]) is aware that the agent is receiving some sort of commission from the third party is likely to preclude the principal from rescinding the transaction with the third party as of right. However, in such circumstances, rescission may still be granted in the court's discretion, and otherwise the principal will retain remedies against the agent.[709] Where the contract between agent and principal provides that the agent may receive commission or other remuneration from the third party and states that where that happens the amount will be disclosed, it is likely to be misleading conduct for the agent not to disclose the actual receipt of commission since the principal may make the assumption that none has been paid.[710]

[705] *Temperley v Blackrod Mfg. Co Ltd* (1907) 71 J.P. 341; *Fiona Trust & Holding Corp v Privalov* [2010] EWHC 3199 (Comm) at [1388].

[706] *Daraydan Holdings Ltd v Solland International Ltd* [2004] EWHC 622 (Ch); [2005] Ch. 119 at [53]. For other cases to the same effect, see below, para.8-222.

[707] *Bartram & Sons v Lloyd* (1904) 90 L.T. 357; *McWilliam v Norton Finance (UK) Ltd (t/a Norton Finance)* [2015] EWCA Civ 186; [2015] 1 All E.R. (Comm) 1026 at [49] (credit broker receives commission from both parties). See also *Christie v McCann* (1972) 27 D.L.R. (3d) 544. The onus is on the agent: *Jordy v Vanderpump* (1920) 64 S.J. 324; *FHR European Ventures LLP v Cedar Capital Partners LLC* [2014] UKSC 45; [2015] A.C. 250.

[708] *Rowland v Chapman* (1901) 17 T.L.R. 669 (knowledge of solicitor imputed).

[709] *Hurstanger Ltd v Wilson* [2007] EWCA Civ 299; [2007] 1 W.L.R. 2351; [2007] 4 All E.R. 1118 (lender pays finder's fee to borrower's agent; loan not rescindable, but agent accountable to borrower). See too *Wood v Commercial First Business Ltd* [2021] EWCA Civ 471; [2021] 3 W.L.R. 395 at [100].

[710] *Wood v Commercial First Business Ltd* [2021] EWCA Civ 471; [2021] 3 W.L.R. 395 at [134], distinguishing *Hurstanger Ltd v Wilson* [2007] EWCA Civ 299.

Remedies

Replace the first paragraph with:

6-087   There are various remedies available to a principal when it discovers that the agent has been bribed. These include parallel remedies at common law and equity. To the extent that a claimant wishes to rely on the common law, it is not necessary for the claimant to plead and prove that the relationship between it and the party bribed was a fiduciary one, although it nearly always will have been.[716a] If the bribe has been paid and is in money, the principal can sue the agent for its amount[717] in an action which was in earlier cases regarded as lying in equity[718] but was subsequently treated as an action in restitution at common law[719]; and this regardless of whether the principal affirms or disaffirms the contract with the third party,[720] and whether the principal has suffered any loss.[721] A sub-agent is similarly liable despite the absence of privity of contract.[722] In this action the person who gave the bribe is also liable jointly and severally.[723] If the bribe is given in property, older cases say that the agent is liable for the value of the property at the highest value which it had while in the agent's possession.[724] Interest is payable from the date when the bribe was received.[725] The Supreme Court has now determined that the proceeds of bribetaking, where identifiable, are held on constructive trust for the principal.[726] This brings English law into line with other common law jurisdictions.[727] This topic is dealt with in more detail above.[728]

[716a] See *Wood v Commercial First Business Ltd* [2021] EWCA Civ 471; [2021] 3 W.L.R. 395 at [102].

[717] *Morison v Thompson* (1874) L.R. 9 Q.B. 480; *Hay's Case* (1875) L.R. 10 Ch.App. 593; *Boston Deep Sea Fishing and Ice Co v Ansell* (1888) 39 Ch.D. 339; *Lister & Co v Stubbs* (1890) 45 Ch.D. 1; *Att.-Gen. v Goddard* (1929) 98 L.J.K.B. 743 (but see Article 48, Illustration 11); *Ardlethan Options Ltd v Easdown* (1916) 20 C.L.R. 285 at 292.

[718] *Fawcett v Whitehouse* (1829) 1 Russ. & M. 132.

[719] *Mahesan v Malaysia Government Officers' Co-operative Housing Society Ltd* [1979] A.C. 374, Illustration 8.

[720] *Logicrose Ltd v Southend United Football Club Ltd* [1988] 1 W.L.R. 1256 at 1263. See too *Marino v FM Capital Partners Ltd* [2020] EWCA Civ 245; [2020] 3 W.L.R. 109.

[721] See *Daraydan Holdings Ltd v Solland International Ltd* [2004] EWHC 622 (Ch); [2005] Ch. 119 at [53].

[722] *Att.-Gen. v Goddard* (1929) 98 L.J.K.B. 743, above; *Powell & Thomas v Evan Jones & Co Ltd* [1905] 1 K.B. 11, Illustration 6 to Article 35; *Daraydan Holdings Ltd v Solland International Ltd* [2004] EWHC 622 (Ch); [2005] Ch. 119 at [52]. A sub-agent may also not be able to plead the head principal's rights as a defence to a claim brought by the sub-principal: see *FM Capital Partners Ltd v Marino* [2018] EWHC 2905 (Comm) at [106] (varied on appeal on other points: [2020] EWCA Civ 245).

[723] *Mahesan's* case [1979] A.C. 374; see Article 78.

[724] *McKay's Case* (1878) 2 Ch.D. 1; *Pearson's Case* (1877) 5 Ch. D. 336; *Nant-y-glo and Blaina Iron Co v Grave* (1878) 12 Ch.D. 738; *Eden v Ridsdales Railway Lamp & Lighting Co Ltd* (1889) 23 Q.B.D. 368; see Illustration 4. It is not clear on what basis a bribe in services would be quantified. An agent will, it seems, be accountable for the market value of a bribe in kind even if the agent asserts that he would not have been willing to pay for the benefit: *Towers v Premier Waste Management Ltd* [2011] EWCA Civ 923 at [48] (use of dumper and excavator on director's private property). See also *Fiona Trust & Holding Corp v Privalov* [2010] EWHC 3199 (Comm) at [1387] (free holiday).

[725] *Nant-y-glo and Blaina Iron Co v Grave* (1878) 12 Ch.D. 738; *Boston Deep Sea Fishing and Ice Co v Ansell* (1888) 39 Ch.D. 339 at 353 and 372 (Illustration 3).

[726] *FHR European Ventures LLP v Cedar Capital Partners LLC* [2014] UKSC 45; [2015] A.C. 250.

[727] See *Att.-Gen. for Hong Kong v Reid* [1994] 1 A.C. 324; *Grimaldi v Chameleon Mining NL (No.2)* (2012) 27 A.L.R. 22.

[728] See above, para.6-042.

Replace footnote 733 with:

[733] *Bulfield v Fournier* (1895) 11 T.L.R. 282; *Swale v Ipswich Tannery Ltd* (1906) 11 Com. Cas. 88; *Temperley v Blackrod Manufacturing Co Ltd* (1907) 71 J.P. 341; *Federal Supply and Cold Storage Co of South Africa v Angehrn & Piel* (1910) 80 L.J.P.C. 1; *Kings Security Systems Ltd v King* [2021] EWHC 325 (Ch) at [204] (rescission of settlement agreement).

RIGHTS OF AGENTS AGAINST THEIR PRINCIPALS

1. REMUNERATION

COMMENT

Fiduciaries

Replace footnote 46 with:

7-006 [46] Including rules made under the Insolvency Act 1986. See too, *Belsner v Cam Legal Services Ltd* [2020] EWHC 2755 (QB) (Solicitors Act 1974).

Unfair Terms in Consumer Contracts Regulations 1999

Replace paragraph with:

7-008 Some commission agreements in consumer contracts may be caught by the Unfair Terms in Consumer Contracts Regulations 1999, for example if a higher sum is due on late payment.[56]

[56] *Bairstow Eves London Central Ltd v Smith* [2004] EWHC 263; [2004] 2 E.G.L.R. 25. But the basic commission charge would not be so subject, by virtue of cl.6(2) of the Regulations. For an example of a penal provision before the Regulations see *Chris Hart (Business Sales) Ltd v Mitchell* 1996 S.C.L.R. 68.

COMMENT

General rule

To the end of the paragraph, add:

7-014 Some types of contingent fee or commission contracts are the subject of regulation.[87a]

[87a] See in relation to those providing litigation services, Courts and Legal Services Act 1990 s.58, and the Damages-Based Agreements Regulations 2013. See also *Cakebread v Fitzwilliam* [2021] EWHC 472 (Comm).

Overpaid commission

Replace footnote 167 with:

7-025 [167] See *Rivoli Hats Ltd v Gooch* [1953] 1 W.L.R. 1190; *Clayton Newbury, Ltd v Findlay* [1953] 1 W.L.R. 1194 (Note); *Bronester Ltd v Priddle* [1961] 1 W.L.R. 1294; *Prudential Assurance Co Ltd v Rodrigues* [1982] 2 N.Z.L.R. 54. See *D.O. Ferguson & Associates v Sohl* (1992) 62 Build.L.R. 95; Birks, in *Consensus ad Idem* (Rose ed., 1996), p.199.

COMMENT

Replace the first paragraph with:

7-028 The principle stated in this Article is no more than a particular example of the wider principle stated in the preceding Article, and it has frequently been noted that there are contracts to which it does not apply.[170] But there exists a body of cases on the notion of "effective cause" which is sufficiently discrete to require segregation. Where the agent is to be remunerated upon the happening of an event, the question whether that event has occurred depends upon the facts of the case and the express or implied terms of the agency contract. Many agents are employed upon terms that if a certain transaction is brought about, they will be entitled to a commission calculated by reference to the amount of the consideration passing in that transaction or to a stated fee. Sometimes the transaction is carried out but has not been brought about as a result of the agent's efforts. Sometimes the agent has played a part in bringing about the transaction but only a small part, or the agent has achieved only a partial success. It can be anticipated that the "effective cause" requirement will be attractive to a court where the agency is not exclusive and there might therefore be multiple agents working independently to secure a transaction.[171]

[170] *Freedman v Union Group Plc* [1997] E.G.C.S. 28; *Raja v Rollerby Ltd* (1997) 74 P. & C.R. D25, per Evans LJ; *Watersheds Ltd v Simms* [2009] EWHC 713 (QB); *Edmond De Rothschild Securities (UK) Ltd v Exillon Energy Plc* [2014] EWHC 2165 (Comm) at [25]; *Eminent Investments (Asia Pacific) Ltd v Dio Corp* [2020] HKCFA 38; (2020) 23 H.K.C.F.A.R. 487 at [71] and [89]; *EMFC Loan Syndications LLP v The Resort Group Plc* [2021] EWCA Civ 844 at [64] and [79].

[171] See *Silvercloud Finance Solutions Ltd (t/a Broadscope Finance) v High Street Solicitors Ltd* [2020] EWHC 878 (Comm) at [93].

"The" or "an"?

Replace footnote 191 with:

[191] *Restatement, Second*, § 448, states that: "an agent is an 'effective cause' ... when his efforts have been sufficiently important in achieving a result for the accomplishment of which the principal has promised to pay him, so that it is just that the principal should pay the promised compensation to him". This definition is open to the objection that it begs the question. But see *Harding Maughan Hambly Ltd v CECAR* [2000] 1 Lloyd's Rep. 316 at 334; *Goh Lay Khim v Isabel Redrup Agency Pte Ltd* [2017] SGCA 11 at [37]; *Winlink Marketing Ltd v The Liverpool Football Club & Athletic Grounds Ltd* [2020] EWHC 2271 (Comm) at [67]. Discussion of the earning of commission is omitted from *Restatement, Third* as being a matter of general contract law.

7-030

Replace footnote 198 with:

[198] *John D. Wood & Co v Dantata* [1987] 2 E.G.L.R. 23; *Chasen Ryder & Co v Hedges* [1993] 1 E.G.L.R. 47; *Outerbridge v Hall* [2020] NSWCA 205. If two different agents are claiming commission from the principal he cannot normally interplead: *Greatorex & Co v Shackle* [1895] 2 Q.B. 249. See also Article 70.

COMMENT

Replace footnote 223 with:

[223] See *Times Travel (UK) Ltd v Pakistan International Airlines Corp* [2021] UKSC 40 (variation not voidable for economic duress).

7-034

3. LIEN

COMMENT

Solicitors' charging lien

Replace footnote 481 with:

[481] *Khans Solicitor (A Firm) v Chifuntwe* [2013] EWCA Civ 481; [2014] 1 W.L.R. 1185; *Gavin Edmondson Solicitors Ltd v Haven Insurance Co Ltd* [2018] UKSC 21; [2018] 1 W.L.R. 2052; *Atkins v Shade Systems Pty Ltd* [2020] NSWSC 1186; (2020) 148 A.C.S.R. 111; *Serious Fraud Office v Litigation Capital Ltd* [2021] EWHC 1272 (Comm) at [374]–[384] (a comprehensive discussion).

7-083

CHAPTER 8

RELATIONS BETWEEN PRINCIPALS AND THIRD PARTIES

1. CONTRACT

COMMENT

Rule (1)

Replace footnote 7 with:

8-002   [7] See, e.g. *Filatona Trading Ltd v Navigator Equities Ltd* [2020] EWCA Civ 109 (where however some of what is said by Simon LJ refers to undisclosed principals, who attract different rules: see below). See also *Humfrey v Dale* (1857) 7 E.&B. 266 at 275 (affirmed (1858) E.B.&E. 1004); *Internaut Shipping GmbH v Fercometal SARL* [2003] 2 Lloyd's Rep. 430 at [56]; *Hamid v Francis Bradshaw Partnership* [2013] EWCA Civ 470; [2013] B.L.R. 447 at [50]–[57]; *Aspen Underwriting Ltd v Kairos Shipping Co Ltd* [2018] EWHC 590; [2019] 1 Lloyd's Rep. 221 at [46] (point not in issue [2020] UKSC 110); *Turks Shipyard Ltd v Owners of the Vessel November* [2020] EWHC 661 (Admlty); *Bell v Ivy Technology Ltd* [2020] EWCA Civ 1563; *Restatement, Third, Agency*, para.6.01 at p.9.

Replace the fourth paragraph with:

In recent cases it has been common to make a reservation for situations referred to above, where the name of the principal is established by extrinsic evidence supplementing or displacing a name in a (usually written) contract, and suggest that the interpretation does not apply where the terms of the contract unequivocally and exhaustively define the parties to it, or some similar phrase.[10] This is plainly connected with the rule excluding the intervention of an undisclosed principal referred to above.[11] The situations are however different.[12] In the undisclosed principal situation the contract is by definition with the agent, and the question is whether its terms are inconsistent with the intervention of another person as principal, bearing in mind that the first or original principal, who turns out to be an agent, is certainly still liable and entitled on the contract. In the disclosed principal situation referred to above, the evidence establishes who the principal is, and (usually) that the agent is not liable: the question is whether there is any clause[13] or other feature of the contract which makes such an interpretation not possible.[14] It has been suggested that this would be difficult to establish.[15] But other authorities conclude that where the document is clear a court should be very reluctant to allow in evidence that will contradict the document.[16] A long line of cases also finds that even where the document refers to the existence of an agency in its heading or recitals, if the signature is unqualified the normal conclusion will be that the signatory is a party.[16a] It can be added that it is undesirable that courts encourage claimants to name as parties to a contract claim persons simply on the basis that they own the subject-matter of the contract or have a legal (e.g. shareholding) or economic connection to the party named in the agreement.[17] It is quite common, for instance, for an asset the subject of a contract to be owned by a party other than the promisor.[18] There should be no presumption that the promisor is the agent, disclosed or undisclosed, of the owner, especially where it is known that the named party is not the owner and the owner has done nothing to encourage a belief that it backs the promise. The owner may have an arrangement with the promisor to pass title to the promisee when the time for performance arrives without being willing to be a party to the contract.

[10] See the *Filatona* case [2020] EWCA Civ 109 at [62].

[11] See the *Filatona* case at first instance, [2019] EWHC 173 (Comm) at [64] where Teare J suggests that substantially the same principle should apply for cases involving disclosed principals.

[12] A complicating feature is that the "beneficial assumption" of Diplock LJ that the third party would normally be prepared to deal with anyone (below, para.8-079) treats all these situations together.

[13] Examples are given in the *Filatona* case at [90]. But "entire agreement" clauses are not necessarily efficacious for either of the above two types of case: see *Aspen Underwriting Ltd v Kairos Shipping Co Ltd* [2018] EWCA Civ 2590; [2019] 1 Lloyd's Rep. 221 at [53] (point not in issue [2020] UKSC 11); *Kaefer Aislamientos SA de CV v AMS Drilling Mexico SA de CV* [2019] EWCA Civ 10; [2019] 1 W.L.R. 3514 at [113].

[14] For a clear explanation of this difference, see the judgment of Males LJ in the *Filatona* case, [2020] EWCA Civ 109.

[15] See the *Filatona* case in the Court of Appeal [2020] EWCA Civ 2590 at [126]; *Bell v Ivy Technology Ltd* [2020] EWCA Civ 1563 at [28].

[16] See *Taylor v Rhino Overseas Inc* [2020] EWCA Civ 353; [2020] Bus. L.R. 1486 at [49]; *Gregor Fisken Ltd v Carl* [2021] EWCA Civ 792; [2021] 4 W.L.R. 91 at [64], explaining the dicta of Jackson LJ in *Hamid v Francis Bradshaw Partnership* [2013] EWCA Civ 470; [2013] Bus. L.R. 447. See also *Barbudev v Eurocom Cable Management Bulgarian Food* [2011] EWHC 1560 (Comm); [2011] 2 All E.R. (Comm) 951 at [114]; and *Americas Bulk Transport Ltd (Liberia) v Cosco Bulk Carrier Ltd (China) MV Grand Fortune* [2020] EWHC 147 (Comm) at [19]; and the discussion in Articles 99 and 100, where the older cases are collected.

[16a] See *Gregor Fisken Ltd v Carl* [2021] EWCA Civ 792; [2021] 4 W.L.R. 91 at [61].

[17] See further above, para.1-030.

[18] See, e.g. *Foster v Action Aviation Ltd* [2014] EWCA Civ 1368 at [38]–[39]; *Taylor v Rhino Overseas Inc* [2020] EWCA Civ 353; [2020] Bus. L.R. 1486 at [51]; *Garnac Grain Co Inc v HMF Faure & Fairclough Ltd* [1968] A.C. 1130; *National Bank of Kazakhstan v Bank of New York Mellon SA/NV* [2020] EWHC 916 (Comm); [2020] 2 B.C.L.C. 726 at [52]. cf. *Turks Shipyard Ltd v Owners of the Vessel November* [2020] EWHC 661 (Admlty) at [16]; *Sotheby's v Mark Weiss Ltd* [2020] EWCA Civ 1570 (co-owners); *Bell v Ivy Technology Ltd* [2020] EWCA Civ 1563 at [26]; *The Swan* [1968] 1 Lloyd's Rep. 5 at 14, Illustration 6 to Article 98 (dealings directly with owner, but see footnote on this case in para.9-034, below).

COMMENT

Applicable outside contract

Replace footnote 48 with:

[48] See, e.g. *Martin v Artyork Investments Ltd* [1997] 2 S.C.R. 290 (apparent authority to borrow, but lender needs also to ensure that draw down is by an authorised person); *Acute Property Developments Ltd v Apostolou* [2013] EWHC 200 (Ch) (manager's authority to direct payment of debt owed to principal to other person); *Pourzand v Telstra Corp Ltd* [2014] WASCA 14 (lessee's property manager authorising lessor to make building alterations); *Lo v Russell* [2016] VSCA 323 (estate agent's apparent authority to receive cooling-off notice); *Active Media Services Inc v Burmester, Duncker & Joly GmbH & Co Kg* [2021] EWHC 232 (Comm) at [268] (estoppel as to compliance by third party with terms of contract).

8-011

Totality of conduct to be looked at

Replace footnote 81 with:

[81] See, e.g. *Kop-Coat New Zealand Ltd v Incodo Ltd* [2018] NZCA 430 at [52] (no holding out of general manager where form of contract contemplated signature of directors); *Stavrinides v Bank of Cyprus*

8-016

Public Co Ltd [2019] EWHC 1328 (Ch) at [107]; *Left Bank Investments Pty Ltd v Ngunya Jarjum Aboriginal Corp* [2020] NSWCA 144 at [109] (holding out contradicted by later evidence).

Ingredients of representation must be sufficient to warrant reliance

Replace footnote 85 with:

8-017
85 See *Rimell v Sampayo* (1824) 1 Car. & P. 253; *Aste v Montague* (1858) 1 F. & F. 264; *Soanes v London and South Western Railway Co* (1919) 88 L.J.K.B. 524.

No representation by agent personally, unless permitted by principal

Replace footnote 97 with:

8-019
97 See *Kelly v Fraser* [2012] UKPC 25; [2013] 1 A.C. 450 at [12]; *Australia and New Zealand Banking Group Ltd v Frenmast Pty Ltd* [2013] NSWCA 459. See further, Watts [2015] L.M.C.L.Q. 36; and P. Watts in W. Day and S. Worthington (eds) *Challenging Private Law* (2020) at pp.258–264. cf. *Allco Finance Group Ltd v Gothard* [2014] FCAFC 6 (director has no apparent authority to communicate more than receivers of company actually decided); *Left Bank Investments Pty Ltd v Ngunya Jarjum Aboriginal Corp* [2020] NSWCA 144 at [109]. See further in relation to companies, para.8-039 below.

On the faith of any such representations

Replace footnote 129 with:

8-023
129 *Tinkler v Revenue & Customs* [2019] EWCA Civ 1392; [2019] 4 W.L.R. 138 at [46] (no intention of using agent as method of serving notice), revsd on appeal on other grounds: [2021] UKSC 39.

COMMENT

Recent developments

Replace footnote 313 with:

8-049
313 *East Asia Co Ltd v PT Satria Tirtatama Energindo* [2019] UKPC 30; [2020] 2 All E.R. 294 (noted I. Sin, "Corporate Contracting, Ostensible Authority and Constructive Notice" (2020) 136 L.Q.R. 364); followed in *Business Mortgage Finance 6 Plc v Roundstone Technologies Ltd* [2019] EWHC 2917 (Ch) at [64]. But see *Harbour Fund III, LP v Kazakhstan Kagazy Plc* [2021] EWHC 1128 (Comm) at [117] (court considered itself bound by ruling in *Quinn v CC Automotive Group Ltd* [2010] EWCA Civ 1412).

Article 76

UNDISCLOSED PRINCIPAL: RIGHTS AND LIABILITIES

Replace list item "(1)" with:

8-068
(1) An undisclosed principal may sue or be sued on a contract made on the principal's behalf, or in respect of money paid or received on his or her behalf, by an agent acting within the scope of the agent's actual authority. Where a contract is involved, the agent on entering into it must have intended to act on the principal's behalf.[393]

393 *Siu Yin Kwan v Eastern Insurance Co Ltd* [1994] 2 A.C. 199 at 207 (Illustration 12), per Lord Lloyd of Berwick; *Taylor v Van Dutch Marine Holding Ltd* [2019] EWHC 1951 (Ch) at [277]; *National Bank of Kazakhstan v Bank of New York Mellon SA/NV* [2020] EWHC 916 (Comm); [2020] 2 B.C.L.C. 726 at [54]. See Comment; Illustrations 1, 2 and 3; *Thomson v Davenport* (1829) 9 B. & C. 78 at 90; *Sims v Bond* (1833) 5 B. & Ad. 389; *Browning v Provincial Insurance Co of Canada* (1873) L.R. 5 P.C. 263 at 272; *Moto Vespa SA v Mat (Britannia Express) Ltd* [1979] 1 Lloyd's Rep. 175. cf. *Restatement, Third*, § 6.03. As to what is an undisclosed principal in this context, see below, para.8-071. As to money paid, see *Duke of Norfolk v Worthy* (1808) 1 Camp. 337, Illustration 3 (action by principal); *Transvaal & Delagoa Bay Investment Co v Atkinson* [1944] 1 All E.R. 579 (liability of principal); Articles 92, 93 and 111. The doctrine is considered against the background of the unsatisfactory drafting of s.14(5) of the Sale of Goods Act 1979 in *Boyter v Thomson* [1995] 2 A.C. 628: see Brown (1996) 112 L.Q.R. 225.

Rule (1): Undisclosed principal doctrine

Replace footnote 412 with:

412 See Pollock (1887) 3 L.Q.R. 358; (1896) 12 L.Q.R. 204; (1898) 14 L.Q.R. 2; Ames (1909) 18 Yale L.J. 443; Lewis (1909) 9 Col.L.Rev. 116; Mechem (1910) 23 HarvL.Rev. 513; Seavey (1920) 29 Yale L.J. 859; Montrose (1938) 16 Can.B.R. 770–771; Weinrib (1975) 21 McGill L.J. 298; Barak (1976) 2 Tel Aviv U. Studies in Law 45; Geva (1979) 25 McGill L.J. 32; Stoljar, pp.228–233; Rochvarg (1989) 34 McGill L.J. 286; Barnett (1987) 75 Calif. L.Rev. 1969; Tan Cheng Han (2004) 120 L.Q.R. 480; G. Fridman, "Undisclosed Principals and the Sale of Goods" in *Agency Law in Commercial Practice* (Busch, Macgregor and Watts eds, 2016), Ch. 5; Tan Cheng Han, "Implied Terms in Undisclosed Agency" (2021) 84 M.L.R. 532.

8-069

Rule (4): Express or implied exclusion of undisclosed principals

Replace footnote 519 with:

519 *Rolls Royce Power Engineering Plc v Ricardo Consulting Engineers Ltd* [2003] EWHC 2871 (TCC); [2004] 2 All E.R. (Comm) 129. For discussion, see P. Watts in W. Day and S. Worthington (eds) *Challenging Private Law* (2020) at pp.265–272; and P. MacMahon, "Contract Law's Transferability Bias" (2020) 95 Indiana L.J. 485.

8-079

Rectification

Replace footnote 617 with:

617 *Hawksford Trustees Jersey Ltd v Stella Global UK Ltd* [2012] EWCA Civ 55; [2012] 2 All E.R. (Comm) 748; *Murray Holdings Investments Ltd v Oscatello Investments Ltd* [2018] EWHC 162 (Ch); *Univar UK Ltd v Smith* [2020] EWHC 1596 (Ch) at [211]; *Liberty Mutual Insurance Company (Australian Branch) v Icon Co (NSW) Pty Ltd* [2021] FCAFC 126 at [317] and [323] (apparent authority may be sufficient).

8-099

General rule

Replace footnote 622 with:

622 *Kymer v Suwercropp* (1807) 1 Camp. 109; *Waring v Favenck* (1807) 1 Camp. 85; *Heald v Kenworthy* (1855) 10 Exch. 739; *Macfarlane v Giannacopulo* (1858) 3 H. & N. 860; *Irvine & Co v Watson & Sons* (1880) 5 Q.B.D. 414; *Chief Executive of NZ Customs Service v Hutchinson* [2021] NZCA 45 at [36].

8-101

Disclosed principal

Replace paragraph with:

Again, in the case of disclosed principal there are clear dicta that where both principal and agent are liable, the third party must elect.[783] The criticisms made above of the merger doctrine for such cases apply a fortiori to any requirement of election. Only if the liabilities are in the alternative does the idea of election make sense[784]; and of the many possible interpretations which can be given to the situation where agent and principal are liable, alternative liability is an unlikely one.[785] In this area however most of the cases appear fairly obviously not to be based on election between two liabilities on an alternative contract at all, but on problems of formation of contract. The typical situation is that discussed in several nineteenth-century cases, where a third party deals with an agent in circumstances where either

8-120

agent or principal might reasonably be regarded as the other contracting party. In principle the law of agency assumes that the third party is dealing with the principal, unless there are clear indications to the contrary,[786] but these there may be.[787] It is also clear that the third party may contract on the basis that both are liable to that party.[788] Thus invoicing and debiting the agent or the like, which are sometimes spoken in terms of election, should perhaps really be classified in terms of offer or counter-offer.[789] There are many cases dealing with this point where the idea of election is not employed at all.[790] Such situations may of course give rise to estoppels as in the case of undisclosed principals. It is therefore submitted that in this area also a supposed election (short of judgment) to have recourse to the agent does not bind the third party unless it again gives rise to some form of estoppel.[791] This does not, of course, remove any authority from the cases referred to above dealing with the question with whom the contract was made.

[783] *Calder v Dobell* (1871) L.R. 6 C.P. 486 at 499 (Illustration 5); *Benton v Campbell Parker & Co* [1925] 2 K.B. 410 at 414; *Murray v Delta Copper Co* [1925] 4 D.L.R. 1061 at 1067; *Tedrick v Big T Restaurants of Canada Ltd* [1983] 2 W.W.R. 135.

[784] *L.C. Fowler & Sons Ltd v St Stephen's College Board of Governors* [1991] 3 N.Z.L.R. 304 at 309 (Illustration 7). See too *Bell v Ivy Technology Ltd* [2020] EWCA Civ 1563 at [37].

[785] See above, para.8-114.

[786] *Thomson v Davenport* (1829) 9 B. & C. 78 at 90.

[787] e.g. *Addison v Gandassequi* (1812) 4 Taunt. 574; cf. *Paterson v Gandasequi* (1812) 15 East 62.

[788] *Calder v Dobell* (1871) L.R. 6 C.P. 486 at 494; Comment to Article 98.

[789] e.g. *Thomson v Davenport* (1829) 9 B. & C. 78. See also cases on building subcontracts: *Young & Co v White* (1911) 28 T.L.R. 87; *Beigtheil & Young v Stewart* (1900) 16 T.L.R. 177; cases on husband and wife: *Jewsbury v Newbold* (1857) 26 L.J.Ex. 247; *Bentley v Griffin* (1814) 5 Taunt. 356; *Metcalfe v Shaw* (1811) 3 Camp. 22; *Callot v Nash* (1923) 39 T.L.R. 292; shipping cases of various sorts: *Eastman v Harry* (1875) 33 L.T. 800; *Whitwell v Perrin* (1858) 4 C.B.(N.S.) 412; *Lamont v Hamilton* 1907 S.C. 628; *Beliard, Crighton (Belgium) & Co Ltd v Charles Lowe & Partners Ltd* (1922) 13 Ll. L. Rep. 567; *The Huntsman* [1894] P. 214; and other cases regularly cited in this connection: *Bottomley v Nuttall* (1858) 5 C.B.(N.S.) 122; *Dramburg v Pollitzer* (1873) 28 L.T. 470; *Re Bowerman Ex p. Vining* (1836) 1 Deac. 555.

[790] e.g. as to husband and wife: *Lea Bridge District Gas Co v Malvern* [1917] 1 K.B. 803; as to ship stores: *Dawson (Ship Stores) v Atlantica Co Ltd* (1931) 40 Ll. L. Rep. 63; *Evans & Reid Coal Co v McNabb, Rougier & Co Ltd* (1924) 18 Ll. L. Rep. 471; *Fraser-Johnston Engineering, etc., Co v Sam Isaacs (Aberdeen) Ltd* (1922) 12 Ll. L. Rep. 233; *Freimuller (Ships Stores) Ltd v Ocean Carriers (London) Ltd* [1961] 2 Lloyd's Rep. 309; *Pearson v Nell* (1860) 12 L.T. 607; *Thompson v Finden* (1829) 4 C. & P. 158. See also *Williamson v Barton* (1862) 7 H. & N. 899; *Gardiner v Heading* [1928] 2 K.B. 284; *Pennell v Alexander* (1854) 3 E. & B. 283; *Thomas v Edwards* (1836) 2 M. & W. 215; *Mortimer v M'Callan* (1840) 6 M. & W. 58 (cf. *Stoneham v Wyman* (1901) 6 Com.Cas. 174); *Format International Security Printers Ltd v Mosden* [1975] 1 Lloyd's Rep. 37. As to ship repairs and stores see Article 99, Illustration 8; Article 101, Illustration 2.

[791] cf. *Restatement, Third*, reporter's notes to § 6.09. See too *Bell v Ivy Technology Ltd* [2020] EWCA Civ 1563 at [37].

2. DISPOSITIONS OF PROPERTY AND RESTITUTIONARY CLAIMS

COMMENT

Replace footnote 831 with:

8-126

[831] *Fielden v Christie-Miller* [2015] EWHC 87 (Ch) at [26]; *Pickering v Hughes* [2021] EWHC 1672 (Ch) at [101].

3. WRONGS

Article 90

LIABILITY OF PRINCIPAL FOR TORTS COMMITTED BY AGENT

Replace list item "(1)" with:

(1) In general,[1113] if an agent is the employee of the principal, the principal is liable for loss, damage or injury caused by the wrongful act of the agent when acting in the course of employment.[1114] Partners are similarly liable for wrongful acts of one another.[1115] **8-177**

[1113] This is an important qualification; see, for instance, torts based on statements, discussed below, para.8-180.

[1114] See Comment: *Salmond and Heuston on the Law of Torts* (21st edn), Ch.21; *Clerk and Lindsell on Torts* (22nd edn), Ch.6; Atiyah, *Vicarious Liability in the Law of Torts* (1967); P. Giliker, *Vicarious Liability in Tort* (2010); P. Giliker "A Revolution in Vicarious Liability" in *Revolution and Evolution in Private Law* (Worthington, Robertson and Virgo eds, 2018), Ch.7. See a not dissimilar formulation in *Restatement, Third*, §7.03. In *New South Wales v Ibbett* (2006) 231 A.L.R. 485 (HCA) exemplary damages were awarded against an employer who was vicariously liable only, see para.8-192, Illustration 7. In *S v Att.-Gen.* [2003] 3 N.Z.L.R. 450 at 472–475 CA (abuse of foster children by foster parents under state control) exemplary damages were held to be generally inappropriate where liability was only vicarious, but the case of abuse of official status was left open. cf. *Kuddus v Chief Constable of Leicestershire Constabulary* [2002] 2 A.C. 122; and *Blackwater v Plint* (2005) 258 D.L.R. (4th) 275 (SCC) (noted Neyers (2006) 122 L.Q.R. 195).

[1115] See Partnership Act 1890 s.10. See *Lindley and Banks on Partnership* (20th edn), Ch.12; and *Dixon Coles & Gill v Baines, Bishop of Leeds* [2021] EWCA Civ 1097 (limitation periods).

COMMENT

Rule (1): Employees and partners

Replace footnote 1123 with:

[1123] See *Holdnerness v Goslin* [1975] 2 N.Z.L.R. 46 at 50–51; *Emmanuel v DBS Management Plc* [1999] **8-178** Lloyd's Rep P.N. 593 at 594. As to Scotland, see *M v Hendron* [2007] CSIH 27 at [132]; *Ryan v Health and Disability Commissioner* [2021] NZCA 347 at [48].

Replace footnote 1139 with:

[1139] *Various Claimants v The Catholic Child Welfare Society* [2012] UKSC 56; [2013] 2 A.C. 1 at [58]; *Barry Congregation of Jehovah's Witnesses v BXB* [2021] EWCA Civ 356; [2021] 4 W.L.R. 42.

Replace footnote 1145 with:

[1145] *Kuwait Asia Bank EC v National Mutual Life Nominees Ltd* [1991] 1 A.C. 187 PC. See also *Uavend Properties Inc v Adsaax Ltd* [2020] EWHC 2073 (Comm) at [60].

Transferred employment

Replace footnote 1155 with:

[1155] *Various Claimants v The Catholic Child Welfare Society* [2012] UKSC 56; [2013] 2 A.C. 1; approving *Viasystems (Tyneside) Ltd v Thermal Transfer (Northern) Ltd* [2005] EWCA Civ 1151; [2005] 4 All **8-179** E.R. 181 (sub-contractor and sub-sub-contractor liable for negligence of employee of subsubcontractor); *Natwest Markets Plc v Bilta (UK) Ltd* [2021] EWCA Civ 680 at [185]. cf. *Day v The Ocean Beach Hotel Shellharbour Pty Ltd* [2013] NSWCA 250; (2013) 85 N.S.W.L.R. 335.

Corporations

Replace paragraph with:

Corporate principals can be liable in tort like individuals, though the torts must **8-189** necessarily be committed through employees or agents. Arguments based on the notion of ultra vires have long been rejected or evaded in the tort context,[1231] and are now removed by legislation which has primary applicability in contract but is also relevant to torts.[1232] Thus corporations can be sued for conversion,[1233] wrongful distress,[1234] false imprisonment,[1235] trespass to land or goods[1236] and, as regards cases where a specific mental element may be involved, defamation,[1237] malicious prosecution,[1238] fraud[1239] and conspiracy.[1240] In general, corporations are liable for the torts of their employees, independent contractors and agents in accordance with the principles already discussed above. The difficulties caused by the use of reasoning that the acts of certain persons may rank as the acts of the corporation itself ("*alter ego*" reasoning) have already been referred to.[1241] Other difficulties arise where it is asserted that a parent company owes direct duties in tort for the activities of its subsidiaries.[1242] Some conduct or omission on the part of the parent company's employees will be required, but it may not be necessary for any formal link such as agency to exist between the two companies.[1243] In principle, the position of a parent company should not be any different from that of a human shareholder who owns the majority or all the shares in the company. Similarly, it makes no difference to the liability in negligence of sellers of products for personal injury or damage to property caused by defects in those products whether the seller is a company or a human.[1243a]

[1231] e.g. *Campbell v Paddington Corp* [1911] 1 K.B. 869.

[1232] Companies Act 2006 ss.39 and 40, considered above, para.8-035 onwards.

[1233] *Yarborough v Bank of England* (1812) 16 East 6; *Giles v Taff Vale Ry* (1853) 2 E. & B. 822; *Barnett v Crystal Palace Co* (1861) 4 L.T. 403.

[1234] *Eastern Counties Ry Co v Broom* (1851) 6 Exch. 314; *Smith v Birmingham Gas Co* (1834) 3 L.J.K.B. 165.

[1235] Illustration 5.

[1236] *Maund v Monmouthshire Canal Co* (1842) 4 Man. & G. 452.

[1237] Illustration 23.

[1238] *Cornford v Carlton Bank* [1899] 1 Q.B. 392.

[1239] *Ranger v Great Western Ry Co* (1854) 5 H.L.Cas. 72; *Barwick v English Joint Stock Bank* (1867) L.R. 2 Ex. 259; *Mackay v Commercial Bank of New Brunswick* (1874) L.R. 5 P.C. 394.

[1240] See *Barclay Pharmaceuticals Ltd v Waypharm LP* [2012] EWHC 306 (Comm); [2013] 2 B.C.L.C. 551 at [229]; *Muduroglu v Reddish LLP* [2015] EWHC 1044 (Ch). But see Watts in *Agency Law in Commercial Practice* (Busch, Macgregor and Watts eds, 2016), p.109.

[1241] See above, paras 1-028 and 8-184.

[1242] See *Chandler v Cape Plc* [2011] EWHC 951 (QB) at [75]; affirmed [2012] EWCA Civ 525; [2012] 1 W.L.R. 3111; *Strategic Formwork Pty Ltd v Hitchen* [2018] NSWCA 54; *Lungowe v Vedanta Resources Plc* [2019] UKSC 20; [2020] A.C. 1045 at [49]; *Okpabi v Royal Dutch Shell Plc* [2021] UKSC 3; [2021] 1 W.L.R. 1294.

[1243] See further para.1-030, above.

[1243a] See *Donoghue v Stevenson* [1932] A.C. 562 (liability on seller, but seller in case was a human).

4. NOTIFICATION TO AND KNOWLEDGE ACQUIRED THROUGH AGENT

COMMENT

Introduction

Replace list item "(a)" with:

8-209   (a) It is always necessary to consider the context of the particular legal issue to which imputation of knowledge might be pertinent. There is no overarching principle that a principal is deemed to know at all times and for all purposes that which an agent knows. In this regard the rules of imputation do not exist in a state of nature, such that some reason has to be found to disapply them.[1366] Hence, a principal might be deemed to possess an agent's knowledge for the purpose of liability to outside parties (or for exposure to regulatory or criminal sanction), but not deemed to know those same facts (let alone have condoned any action by the agent) for the purpose of action by the principal against the agent personally.[1367] Further, a distinction needs to be drawn between imputation of knowledge in the context of the formation or execution of a contract between arm's length parties, and imputation in the context of the imposition of tortious or restitutionary liability. Cases of the former sort turn on the express or implied understandings between the parties, and, in the absence of express agreement, can usually be reduced to determining what a party could reasonably expect the counterparty to know, given the state of knowledge of their respective agents.[1368] This type of case is always very fact specific. Certainly, the principles of apparent authority cannot be end run by the third party asserting that the principal is bound to a contract as a result of being deemed to know of the unauthorised conduct of its undoubted employees or agents.[1369] Cases in tort and restitution, on the other hand, involve *imposed* obligations, and require the law to formulate relatively firm principles. The liability in tort of principals mostly turns on vicarious liability and not on imputing knowledge, but the issue could arise in an action in negligence (did the principal know that the product was dangerous?) or negligent misstatement. The issue might also be relevant to defences, whether or not the party with knowledge is strictly an agent. For instance, the knowledge of an employee who has no agency functions might be imputed to an employer and preclude an action in tort by the employer.[1370] Questions of the knowledge of agents do, however, play a particularly prominent role in restitutionary liability, either as an element of the cause of action or as a factor in the application of defences.[1371] It has been argued that given that most restitutionary claims are bounded by the value that has been received by the defendant, one might expect the rules for imputation to be somewhat more liberal than in tort.[1372] There can be cases of a third sort, where the operation of a statutory rule turns on the state of a party's knowledge. There, it is a question of statutory construction what rules of imputation were intended; the context of the provision will be highly relevant, as in the contractual context, but the inference may also be that the legislature intended to borrow the rules used in tortious and restitutionary situations.[1373] Normally, however, it is unsatisfactory to borrow case law from one context for use in another.

[1366] A passage approved in *Bilta (UK) Ltd v Nazir (No.2)* [2015] UKSC 23; [2016] A.C. 1 at [44] and [191]. See also *Moulin Global Eyecare Trading Ltd v CIR* [2014] HKCFA 22 at [106], per Lord Walker of Gestingthorpe; *HKSAR v Luk Kin* [2016] HKCFA 81 at [41], per Lord Hoffmann.

[1367] See *Bilta (UK) Ltd v Nazir (No.2)* [2015] UKSC 23; [2016] A.C. 1 at [7], [43], and [208]; *Mobile Sourcing Ltd v Revenue and Customs Commissioners* [2016] UKUT 274 (TCC) at [48]; *Faichney v Aquila Advisory Ltd* [2018] EWHC 565 (Ch) at [53].

[1368] See *Jafari-Fini v Skillglass Ltd* [2007] EWCA Civ 261 at [97], per Moore-Bick LJ, Illustration 20; *Bilta (UK) Ltd v Nazir (No.2)* [2015] UKSC 23; [2016] A.C. 1 at [198]; *Hut Group Ltd v Nobahar-Cookson* [2014] EWHC 3842 (QB) at [226]; affirmed on other points [2016] EWCA Civ 128. For an example where, as a matter of construction, imputation was found inapplicable, see *Infiniteland Ltd v Artisan Contracting Ltd* [2005] EWCA Civ 758; [2006] 1 B.C.L.C. 632.

1369 See, e.g. *Taylor v Smith* (1926) 38 C.L.R. 48, Article 16, Illustration 8.

1370 See, e.g. *Howmet Ltd v Economy Devices Ltd* [2016] EWCA Civ 847; (2016) 168 Con. L.R. 27 at [72] and [95] (claimant fails in tort action in respect of losses caused by defective product when its employee became aware of defect).

1371 On this, see P. Watts, "The Acts and States of Knowledge of Agents as Factors in Principals' Restitutionary Liability" [2017] L.M.C.L.Q. 385. See also *Lewski v Commissioner of Taxation* [2017] FCAFC 145 at [142] (agent's knowledge forecloses right to disclaim property); *Knightsbridge Property Development Corp (UK) Ltd v South Chelsea Properties Ltd* [2017] EWHC 2730 (Ch) (imputed knowledge of wrongful removal of charge and transfer of land). As to imputation in rectification actions, see above, para.8-099.

1372 See Watts [2017] L.M.C.L.Q. 385.

1373 See, e.g. *Meridian Global Funds Management Asia Ltd v Securities Commission* [1995] 2 A.C. 500; *G-Star Raw CV v Rhodi Ltd* [2015] EWHC 216 (Ch) at [167] (civil liability for knowingly importing items that infringe copyright); *Jeanswest Corp (New Zealand) Ltd v G-Star Raw CV* [2015] NZCA 14 at [111] (copyright); *Reformation Publishing Co Ltd v Cruiseco Ltd* [2018] EWHC 2761 (Ch) (aggravated damages for breach of copyright); *Julien v Evolving Technologies and Enterprise Development Co Ltd* [2018] UKPC 2 (concept of "discovery" of facts by company for purposes of statute of limitations); *Sandham v Revenue and Customs Commissioners* [2020] UKUT 193 (TCC) at [14].

Rule (1): Rationales for imputation

Replace footnote 1398 with:

8-210   1398 See *Espin v Pemberton* (1859) 3 De G. & J. 547 at 555; *Rolland v Hart* (1871) L.R. 6 Ch.App. 678 at 681–682; *Boursot v Savage* (1866) L.R. 2 Eq. 134 at 142; *Active Media Services Inc v Burmester, Duncker & Joly GmbH & Co Kg* [2021] EWHC 232 (Comm) at [266]. For other cases not supporting the presumption as the basis of imputation, see (2001) 117 L.Q.R. 300 at 304–308.

Only knowledge acquired while performing mandate prima facie imputed

Replace the first paragraph with:

8-211   It is implicit in Rule (1) that only knowledge acquired by an agent whilst carrying out tasks for the principal will be imputed.[1401] Knowledge acquired when not acting for the principal, whether acquired before or even during the period of appointment, would not be imputed. Such an approach has been taken in decisions over many years[1402]; though it is rejected by both *Restatement, Second* and *Restatement, Third*.[1403] Rule (1) is consistent with either general rationale discussed in the previous paragraph, but arguably not dictated by them. Another explanation that has been given from time to time, particularly in priority disputes and other restitutionary contexts, is that it is unreasonable to expect a busy agent, such as a solicitor, to recall all information that might be relevant to a client's affairs when it was learned while acting for other clients. This rationale emerged early in judgments of Lord Harwicke LC, in particular *Warrick v Warrick*[1404]:

> "[N]otice should be in the same transaction: this rule ought to be adhered to, otherwise it would make purchasers and mortgagees' titles depend altogether on the memory of their counsellors and agents, and oblige them to apply to persons of less eminence as counsel, as not being so likely to have notice of former transactions."

This led some later judges to suggest that if two matters for separate principals took place so close to one another that the knowledge acquired in the first matter must have been still present in the agent's mind, imputation could occur. So, Lord Eldon LC stated in *Mountford v Scott*[1405]:

> "The Vice-Chancellor in this case appears to have proceeded upon the notion that notice to a man in one transaction is not to be taken as notice to him in another transaction; in

that view of the case it might fall to be considered, whether one transaction might not follow so close upon the other, as to render it impossible to give a man credit for having forgotten it. I should be unwilling to go so far as to say, that if an attorney has notice of a transaction in the morning, he shall be held in a Court of Equity to have forgotten it in the evening; it must in all cases depend upon the circumstances."

The tendency nonetheless has been to conform to the understanding that knowledge needs to have been acquired by the agent whilst acting for the principal.[1406] There are, however, some very important notes and qualifications that need to be made about Rule (1). First, the rule is about knowledge acquired by an agent outside any agency for the principal, so that imputation could still occur where the knowledge was acquired while acting for the same principal, albeit in an earlier transaction (subject to issues of forgetfulness).[1407] It will be seen below that there is an important statutory exception to that position. Secondly, the knowledge of an agent who is acting for more than one party to the same transaction is not generally compartmentalised, and is likely to be imputed to both (or more) principals.[1408] There may be circumstances where the agent's duties of confidentiality might provide a reason for not imputing the knowledge to both principals,[1409] but where the knowledge relates to the position of some outside claimant (e.g. possession of an equitable interest in an asset) it is unlikely that the agent's duties of confidentiality could justify prejudicing the position of that party. Thirdly, courts will be resistant to arguments that two connected transactions were nonetheless discrete for the purposes of the rules of imputation. Fourthly, the rule is, in any event, only a starting point. Most of the cases that created the rule have involved solicitors, the scope of whose authority is normally limited. Other case law suggests that where an agent is given responsibility for the carriage of the transaction at issue, the principal may be burdened with whatever knowledge the agent possesses wherever acquired. For example, if it is only through the auspices of the agent that the principal could have obtained the property or rights that are now contested by the claimant, it would be wrong to allow the principal to adopt the agent's actions whilst disowning the agent's knowledge of the claimant's prior rights.[1410] The well-known dictum of Lord Halsbury LC in *Blackburn, Low & Co v Vigors* provides support for such an approach[1411]:

> "Some agents so far represent the principal that in all respects their acts and intentions and their knowledge may truly be said to be the acts, intentions, and knowledge of the principal. Other agents may have so limited and narrow an authority both in fact and in the common understanding of their form of employment that it would be quite inaccurate to say that such an agent's knowledge or intentions are the knowledge or intentions of his principal ...".

This would provide an explanation for the actual result in the *El Ajou* case, itself a case concerned with knowledge acquired outside the agency, and more convincing than the reasoning actually used in that case, which was to fashion a special rule for companies.[1412] Hoffmann LJ alluded to other situations where a principal can be affected by an agent's knowledge acquired before or outside the agency. These are also somewhat problematic and are the subject of Rules (2) and (3).[1413]

[1401] For discussion, see Watts [2005] N.Z.L. Rev. 307; Watts [2017] L.M.C.L.Q. 385.

[1402] See, e.g. *Taylor v Yorkshire Insurance Co Ltd* [1913] 2 Ir.R. 1 at 21 and other cases there cited; *Mountford v Scott* (1818) 3 Madd. 34 at 40; *Williamson v Barbour* (1877) 9 Ch.D. 529 (knowledge of new partner that defendant had been defrauding firm not imputed); *El Ajou v Dollar Land Holdings Ltd* [1994] 2 All E.R. 685; *Farah Constructions Pty Ltd v Say-Dee Pty Ltd* (2007) 236 C.L.R. 89 at [125] (assumption by court that only knowledge acquired within mandate is imputable); *Hickman v Turn and*

Wave Ltd [2011] 3 N.Z.L.R. 318 at [192]; reversed on other grounds [2013] 1 N.Z.L.R. 741; *Steel Co Ltd v Pipes NZ Ltd* [2016] NZCA 175 at [28] (knowledge of counterparty's standard terms acquired when agent was acting for former owner of business not carried forward to new owner).

1403 See *Restatement, Third*, § 5.03.

1404 *Warrick v Warrick* (1745) 3 Atk. 291 at 293. See also *Preston v Tubbin* (1684) 1 Vern. 286; *Worsley v The Earl of Scarborough* (1746) 3 Atk. 392: "It is settled, that notice to an agent or counsel who was employed in the thing by another person, or in another business, and at another time, is no notice to his client, who employs him afterwards; and it would be very mischievous if was so, for the man of most practice and greatest eminence would then be the most dangerous to employ".

1405 *Mountford v Scott* (1818) 3 Madd. 34. See also *Hargreaves v Rothwell* (1836) 1 Keen 154; *Williamson v Barbour* (1877) 9 Ch.D. 529 at 535; *Burnard v Lysnar* [1927] N.Z.L.R. 757.

1406 See *Fuller v Benett* (1843) 2 Hare 394; *O'Keefe v London & Edinburgh Insurance Co Ltd* [1928] N.I. 85 at 97, per Andrews LJ: "The danger of making the agent's memory of bygone transactions a jury question is obvious, and recollection or forgetfulness by the agent of matters known to him previous to that relation is not allowed to affect the liability of the principal except in certain well-recognised cases".

1407 See *Brotherton v Hatt* (1706) 2 Vern. 574; *Jennings v Moore* (1708) 2 Vern. 609; affirmed sub nom. *Blenkarne v Jennens* (1709) 2 Bro. P.C. 278 HL; *Le Neve v Le Neve* (1748) 1 Ves. Sen. 64; (1748) 3 Atk. 646; *Doe d. Willis v Martin* (1790) 4 T.R. 39; *Rolland v Hart* (1871) L.R. 6 Ch.App. 678; *Left Bank Investments Pty Ltd v Ngunya Jarjum Aboriginal Corp* [2020] NSWCA 144 at [103].

1408 In addition to the cases in the preceding footnote, see *Dresser v Norwood* (1864) 17 C.B.(N.S.) 466; *Boursot v Savage* (1866) L.R. 2 Eq. 134; *Belmont Finance Corp v Williams Furniture Ltd (No.2)* [1980] 1 All E.R. 393 at 404 (common director); *Bank of Credit and Commerce International SA v Aboody* [1990] 1 Q.B. 923 at 974–975; *David Browne Contractors Ltd v Petterson* [2017] NZSC 116; [2018] 1 N.Z.L.R. 112 at [121]; *Active Media Services Inc v Burmester, Duncker & Joly GmbH & Co Kg* [2021] EWHC 232 (Comm) at [266]. See also the cases in fn.1413 below.

1409 See *Harkness v Commonwealth Bank of Australia Ltd* (1993) 32 N.S.W.L.R. 543 at 555.

1410 See, e.g. *Jessett Properties Ltd v UDC Finance Ltd* [1992] 1 N.Z.L.R. 138; *Permanent Trustee Australia Co Ltd v FAI General Insurance Co Ltd* (2001) 50 N.S.W.L.R. 679 at 692–697 (reversed on other issues (2003) 214 C.L.R. 514). cf. *Cassegrain v Gerard Cassegrain & Co Pty Ltd* [2015] HCA 2; (2015) 254 C.L.R. 425 at [41] (where the defendant was (puzzlingly) held to be the purely passive recipient of property, deputing no agency tasks to obtain it).

1411 *Blackburn, Low & Co v Vigors* (1887) 12 App. Cas. 531 at 537–538. See too *Brittain v Brown* (1871) 24 L.T. 504 at 506, per Cockburn CJ: "I quite agree that where a man employs an attorney or agent, and places him in his own place and treats him as alter ego, there the doctrine contended for would apply, viz., that a principal is bound by the knowledge of his agent. But it is very different when the contract itself is not placed in the hands of an agent, but the agent is, as here, employed about a matter entirely subsidiary and accessory to the contract"; *Grand Trunk Railway Co of Canada v Robinson* [1915] A.C. 740 at 747.

1412 *El Ajou v Dollar Land Holdings Ltd* [1994] 2 All E.R. 685 at 705, Illustration 16. See further below, para.8-215.

1413 e.g. Illustrations 7–11 and 15; and *Bank of Credit and Commerce International SA v Aboody* [1990] 1 Q.B. 923 at 974–975. But see Law of Property Act 1925 s.199(i)(ii), below, para.8-216.

Rule (4): Claims by principal against own agent, and fraud of agent

Replace the second paragraph with:

8-214   The first relates to complaints by a principal that an agent has broken duties owed the principal; the claim may be against the agent, or a third party which has promoted[1443] or otherwise assisted in, or benefited from, the breach.[1444] Or the claim may be against a third party whose very duty was to detect the fraud or other misconduct of the agent.[1445] The principal is then met with an allegation that the principal must be deemed to have known what the agent knew or has done, and by inference to have condoned the agent's actions. The fraud exception has been used to reject this argument. This version of the exception is often associated with *Re Hampshire Land Co*,[1446] although the facts of the case do not in fact furnish a good example of it. It is not surprising that defences of this sort have been routinely rejected,[1447] for they have no merit. However, it is suggested that to invoke a fraud exception to deal with them is misconceived. First, there is no reason to limit the "exception" to fraudulent breaches of duty. If this defensive argument had had any merit it would have been equally applicable to honest breaches of duty. The simple point is that, were the principal deemed to possess an agent's knowledge of the agent's own breaches of duty, and thereby to have condoned them, the principal could never successfully vindicate his or her rights.[1448] Secondly, there is no need for an exception as such. The putative defence that the exception is used to rebut is premised on the fallacy that a principal is prima facie deemed to know at all times and for all purposes that which his agents know. As observed already, imputation has never operated in such a way.[1449] Before imputation occurs, there needs to be some purpose for deeming the principal to know what the agent knows. There is none in this type of case. Reasoning of this sort has now been adopted in the *Bilta* case; there is no exception, rather there is no reason to impute knowledge in these cases.[1450] *Bilta* itself is an example of a case where the underlying fraud was directed at a third party (the Revenue) and not at the principal (a company), but it was held that attribution of that wrongdoing to the principal for some purposes would not preclude the principal from suing its dishonest agents and associates in order to rectify the wrong done to the third party.[1450a]

[1443] See *Wells v Smith* [1914] 3 K.B. 722 at 726, per Scrutton J: "[A] man who tells a lie to another cannot protect himself by saying 'Your agent should have warned you of my lie'" (defendant to deceit action cannot rely on fact one dishonest agent of claimant knew of the untruth); *Renault UK Ltd v Fleetpro Technical Services Ltd* [2007] EWHC 2541 (QB); [2008] Bus. L.R. D17 at [124]; *OMV Petrom SA v Glencore International AG* [2015] EWHC 666 (Comm) at [152] (affirmed on different points, [2016] EWCA Civ 778).

[1444] See *Brinks-Mat Ltd v Noye* [1991] 1 Bank L.R. 68; *Nationwide Building Society v Dunlop Haywards Ltd* [2007] EWHC 1374 (Comm) (action in deceit); *Bilta (UK) Ltd v Nazir (No.2)* [2015] UKSC 23; [2016] A.C. 1 at [95], [207]; *Burnden Holdings (UK) Ltd v Fielding* [2016] EWCA Civ 557; [2017] 1 W.L.R. 39 at [49]; affirmed on different points [2018] UKSC 14; [2018] A.C. 857 (knowledge of dishonest agents not imputed for purposes of limitation period in action by principal); *UBS AG (London Branch) v Kommunale Wasserwerke Peipkiz GmbH* [2017] EWCA Civ 1567 at [151]; *Singularis Holdings Ltd v Daiwa Capital Markets Europe Ltd* [2019] UKSC 50; [2019] 3 W.L.R. 997 at [34]; *Skandinaviska Enskilda Banken AB (Publ) v Conway* [2019] UKPC 36 at [124].

[1445] See *Singularis Holdings Ltd v Daiwa Capital Markets Europe Ltd* [2019] UKSC 50; [2019] 3 W.L.R. 997 at [34] (albeit that the *Quincecare* duty is not an obvious one: see above, para.5-016). The position will be different if all the persons to whom the duty was owed were complicit in the misconduct: this is the best explanation of the result in *Stone & Rolls Ltd v Moore Stephens (A Firm)* [2009] UKHL 39; [2009] 1 A.C. 1391.

[1446] [1896] 2 Ch. 743, Illustration 21. See note to Illustration 21 below, and Watts (2001) 117 L.Q.R. 300 at 319–320 and in *Unjust Enrichment in Commercial Law* (Degeling and Edelman eds, 2008), Ch.21.

[1447] See *Sharpe v Foy* (1868) L.R. 4 Ch.App. 35; *Re Fitzroy Bessemer Steel Co Ltd* (1884) 50 L.T. 144, Illustration 9; *Houghton v Nothard, Lowe & Wills* [1928] A.C. 1; *Belmont Finance Corp v Williams Furniture Ltd* [1979] Ch. 250; *Nationwide Building Society v Dunlop Haywards Ltd* [2007] EWHC 1374 (Comm) at [75]; *Moore Stephens v Stone & Rolls Ltd* [2008] EWCA Civ 644; [2009] 1 A.C. 1391; [2008] 2 Lloyd's Rep. 319; [2008] 2 B.C.L.C. 461 at [71]–[72]; affirmed [2009] UKHL 39; [2009] 1 A.C. 1391; *Soods Solicitors v Dormer* [2010] EWHC 502 (QB); *Moulin Global Eyecare Trading Ltd v CIR* [2014] HKCFA 22 at [106]; *Grimaldi v Chameleon Mining NL (No.2)* (2012) 287 A.L.R. 22 at [285]; *JSC BTA Bank v Ablyazov* [2013] EWHC 510 (Comm) at [166]; *Faichney v Aquila Advisory Ltd* [2018] EWHC 565 (Ch) at [55].

[1448] See *Stone & Rolls Ltd v Moore Stephens Ltd* [2009] UKHL 39; [2009] 1 A.C. 1391 at [198]; *Tonto Home Loans Australia Pty Ltd v Tavares* [2011] NSWCA 389 at [209]. See further Watts (2001) 117 L.Q.R. 300 at 316–318. See now *Bilta (UK) Ltd v Nazir (No.2)* [2015] UKSC 23; [2016] A.C. 1 at [7], [202].

[1449] cf. *El Ajou v Dollar Land Holdings Plc* [1994] 2 All E.R. 685 at 715, per Hoffmann LJ: "English law has never taken the view that the knowledge of a director [is] ipso facto imputed to the company—see *Powles v Page* (1846) 3 C.B. 16".

[1450] *Bilta (UK) Ltd v Nazir (No.2)* [2015] UKSC 23; [2016] A.C. 1 at [9], [37], [181].

[1450a] See also *Brink's-Mat Ltd v Noye* [1991] 1 Bank L.R. 68; *Young v Murphy* (1994) 13 A.C.S.R. 722; *Dalriada Trustees Ltd v Woodward* [2012] EWHC 21626 (Ch); *Nicholson Street Pty Ltd v Letten* [2016]

VSCA 157. cf *Break Fast Investments Pty Ltd v Rigby Cooke Lawyers (A Firm)* [2021] VSC 398 at [350] (no evidence that principal attempting to cure breach).

Agents of companies and large organisations

Replace the second paragraph with:

8-215   An issue that has arisen quite frequently, but once more without clear resolution, is the situation where one director of a company knows a relevant fact but others do not. The same issue could arise with other organisations that use committees. The starting point seems to be that knowledge held by one director relevant to the position of a third party will generally be imputed to the company.[1469] This may reflect the general idea that the more senior the agent the less appropriate it is to permit the principal to disown inconvenient knowledge. But this is only a starting point, and as usual the question turns on the issue at stake. The same categories of case as are discussed in the preceding paragraph need to be considered. So, in restitutionary claims, a single director's knowledge is likely to be imputed to the recipient company.[1469a] On the other hand, where it is an issue of a wrong done to a company in respect of which the company is now claiming, the knowledge of a director implicated in the wrongdoing would not be imputed for the purposes of defeating the claim; imputation in such circumstances would operate as a rogue's charter. Similarly, in the context of the creation and performance of contracts, it may in the particular context be unreasonable for one party to assert that the other knew something, let alone agreed to something, by reason of one director's knowledge.[1470] In the context of consent to an agent's receiving what would otherwise be a secret commission, usually that consent would need to be given by someone more senior than the recipient[1471]; where the recipient is a director that may require that the consent be given by the board and even in some circumstances by the shareholders, and those persons will need to know the facts. There can be other reasons for not imputing the knowledge of one or more directors. In two well-known cases where imputation did not occur the knowledge related to a matter that was only tangential to a claim being brought by the relevant company. In particular, the defendant, also a company, wanted to deny liability on a contract of loan because it asserted that its management was intending to use the proceeds for ultra vires activity, and that one of the lender's directors, being also a director of the borrower, was aware of the intended use of the funds.[1472] It is, perhaps, not surprising that imputation did not occur in those circumstances. These cases do not create a general principle, contrary to the assumption made in *El Ajou*. In a third case, the issue of law related to the giving of notice, not knowledge, and it was held that no notice was given to a company, Co B, which shared a common officer with the party that might have given notice, Co A, in circumstances where Co A had no wish to give a notice.[1473]

[1469] See *Belmont Finance Corp v Williams Furniture Ltd (No.2)* [1980] 1 All E.R. 393 at 404; *Marr v Arabco Traders Ltd* (1987) 1 N.Z. Business L.C. 102,732; *ZBB (Australia) Ltd v Allen* (1991) 4 A.C.S.R. 495 at 506–507; *Farrow Finance Co Ltd v Farrow Properties Pty Ltd* (1998) 26 A.C.S.R. 544 at 587; *Jafari-Fini v Skillglass Ltd* [2007] EWCA Civ 261 at [98]; *Lebon v Aqua Salt Co Ltd* [2009] UKPC 2 at [26]; *Tonto Home Loans Australia Pty Ltd v Tavares* [2011] NSWCA 389 at [212]; *Stockman Interhold SA v Arricano Real Estate Plc* [2017] EWHC 2909 (Comm) at [198] (non-executive director).

[1469a] But see *Li v 110 Formosa NZ Ltd* [2020] NZCA 492 at [145] (director a minority shareholder with no executive role).

[1470] See, e.g. *Sycamore Bidco Ltd v Breslin* [2012] EWHC 3443 (Ch) at [388] (directors of company the shares of which were being sold became directors of purchaser; knowledge of transferred directors not imputed to preclude purchaser from complaining about breaches of warranty and misrepresentations made by and on behalf of seller); *Jafari-Fini v Skillglass Ltd* [2007] EWCA Civ 261 at [97]; *PEC Ltd v Asia Golden Rice Co Ltd* [2014] EWHC 1583 (Comm) at [58] (majority of board's knowledge of more junior employee's actions did not bind company where formal resolution of board needed for actual authority); *Sanpoint Pty Ltd v V8 Supercars Holding Pty Ltd* [2019] NSWCA 5.

[1471] See *Ross River Ltd v Cambridge City Football Club Ltd* [2007] EWHC 2115 (Ch) at [213]; *BFS Group Ltd v Foley* [2017] EWHC 2799 (QB) at [29]. See further, para.6-086, above.

[1472] *Re Marseilles Extension Railway Co Ex p. Crédit Foncier and Mobilier of England* (1871) L.R. 7 Ch.App. 161; *Re David Payne & Co Ltd* [1904] 2 Ch. 608. See the discussion in Watts [2005] N.Z.L. Rev. 307 at 329. As for *Re Hampshire Land Co* [1896] 2 Ch. 743, Illustration 21, see fn.1512, below.

[1473] *Re Fenwick, Stobart & Co, Deep Sea Fishery Co's Claim* [1902] 1 Ch. 507 (notice of dishonour of a bill of exchange).

ILLUSTRATIONS

Replace list item "(11)" with:

(11) A solicitor who was employed to transfer a mortgage knew that there were incumbrances on the property subsequent to such mortgage. Held, that his knowledge did not operate as notice of the incumbrances to the transferee, because the incumbrances were not material to the transfer, for which alone the solicitor was employed.[1501]   **8-217**

[1501] *Wyllie v Pollen* (1863) 32 L.J.Ch. 782; *Brittain v Brown & Millar* (1871) 24 L.T. 504 (solicitor had drafting role only). See also *Wythes v Labouchere* (1859) 3 De G. & J. 593; *Wells v Smith* [1914] 3 K.B. 722; *Wilkinson v General Accident, etc., Corp* [1967] 2 Lloyd's Rep. 182; *The Hayle* [1929] P. 275.

5. INTERFERENCE WITH AGENT BY THIRD PARTY AND INVOLVEMENT IN AGENT'S BREACH OF DUTY

COMMENT

Bribery and secret commissions

Replace paragraph with:

Bribery is a particularly obvious form of corruption, and one that has attracted much attention since the nineteenth century from both common law and equity. A small group of core cases before and after the beginning of the twentieth century lay down and repeat stern rules in respect of bribery, which dominate the area and appear to have had some element of deterrent purpose. Definitions of bribery and of the wider concept of a secret commission, together with an account of the internal effect of the applicable rules as between principal and agent have been addressed in Article 49. This Article concerns the external effect, but should be read in conjunction with the commentary to Article 49. The breadth of the concept of a secret commission means that a third party who offers or confers money or some other personal benefit on an agent cannot escape legal repercussions merely because the third party avers that he or she thought that the agent would tell or had told the principal of the payment[1544]; or was unaware of the agent's exact intention but aware that the agent did not intend to disclose the dealing to the principal.[1545] The third party is also liable where having arranged for the payment not knowing of the agency, that party continued and entered into the contract with the principal after he or she had learned of it.[1546] It is not necessary for the principal to show that the third party had an intention to influence the agent.[1547] Although it is true that the objectionable feature of bribery is the general one that it gives rise to a conflict of interest,[1548] factors such as those above distinguish bribes from the more general idea of undisclosed profit, which need not involve the complicity of a third party.[1549]   **8-222**

[1544] *Shipway v Broadwood* [1899] 1 Q.B. 369 at 373 (Illustration 3); *Grant v Gold Exploration and Development Syndicate Ltd* [1900] 1 Q.B. 233 at 248–250; *Taylor v Walker* [1958] 1 Lloyd's Rep. 490,

Illustration 4, at 509–513; *Daraydan Holdings Ltd v Solland International Ltd* [2004] EWHC 622 (Ch); [2005] Ch. 119 at [53]; *Otkritie International Investment Management Ltd v Urumov* [2014] EWHC 191 (Comm) at [68]; *Shagang Shipping Co Ltd v HNA Group Co Ltd* [2018] EWCA Civ 1732 at [84] (intention to influence need not be shown); reversed on the facts [2020] UKSC 34; *Pengelly v Business Mortgage Finance 4 Plc* [2020] EWHC 2002 (Ch) at [55] and [78] (affd *Wood v Commercial First Business Ltd* [2021] EWCA Civ 471; [2021] 3 W.L.R. 395 on different points).

1545 *Logicrose Ltd v Southend United FC* [1988] 1 W.L.R. 1256 at 1260–1262.

1546 *Grant v Gold Exploration and Development Syndicate Ltd* [1900] 1 Q.B. 233 at 248.

1547 *Industries and General Mortgage Co Ltd v Lewis* [1949] 2 All E.R. 573.

1548 *Anangel Atlas Cla. Naviera SA v Ishikawajima-Harima Heavy Industries Co Ltd* [1990] 1 Lloyd's Rep. 167 at 171.

1549 As to secret profits, see Articles 45–47.

Forms of relief and remedy

Replace footnote 1551 with:

8-223   1551 See *Hurstanger Ltd v Wilson* [2007] EWCA Civ 299; [2007] 1 W.L.R. 2351; [2007] 4 All E.R. 1118 at [47]. See too above, para.6-085. cf. *Wood v Commercial First Business Ltd* [2021] EWCA Civ 471; [2021] 3 W.L.R. 395 at [134] (undertaking to disclose payments from third party not kept, so rescission the appropriate remedy).

RELATIONS BETWEEN AGENTS AND THIRD PARTIES

1. CONTRACT

COMMENT

Agent may be liable or entitled

Replace footnote 22 with:

9-005   [22] *Montgomerie v UK Mutual SS Assn* [1891] 1 Q.B. 370 at 372, per Wright J (in a later part of the judgment some of which is cited in para.9-002 above). See also *Fawkes v Lamb* (1862) 31 L.J.Q.B. 98 at 100; *The Swan* [1968] 1 Lloyd's Rep. 5, Illustration 6; *Carminco Gold & Resources Ltd v Findlay & Co Stockbrokers (Underwriters) Pty Ltd* (2007) 243 A.L.R. 472, Illustration 24 to Article 98; *Felty v Ernst & Young LLP* [2015] BCCA 445; *Tattersalls Ltd v McMahon* [2021] EWHC 1629 (QB).

COMMENT

Replace list with:

9-037   (a)   If the contract is signed by the agent personally without qualification, the agent is deemed to have contracted personally[245] unless a contrary intention plainly appears from other portions of the document.[246]

(b)   The mere fact that the agent is described as an agent, director, secretary, manager, broker, etc. whether by words connected with or forming part of the signature,[247] or in the body of the contract,[248] and whether or not the principal is named, raises no presumption that the agent did not intend to contract personally; but here again an intention to contract as agent only may be gathered from the whole document and surrounding circumstances.[249] More weight will normally be given to the description accompanying the signature than to references in the heading or recitals to the document.[249a]

(c)   But if the agent adds to a signature words indicating that he or she signs as agent, or for or on behalf or on account of a principal, the agent is deemed not to have contracted personally,[250] unless it is plain from other portions of the document that, notwithstanding such qualified signature, the agent intended to be bound.[251] This is so even though the principal is unnamed.[252] But this proposition should be read subject to Article 102(2) regarding the liability of agents under trade custom.

[245] Illustration 5. And see *Lavan v Walsh* [1964] I.R. 87; and *Transcontinental Underwriting Agencies Srl v Grand Union Insurance Co Ltd* [1987] 2 Lloyd's Rep. 409, where this formulation is approved; *Farncombe v Sperling* (1922) 66 S.J. 312; *Ernest Scragg & Son Ltd v Perserverance Banking and Trust Co Ltd* [1973] 2 Lloyd's Rep. 101; *Sika Contracts Ltd v B.S. Gill* (1978) 9 Build. L.R. 11, Illustration 10; *Rebnik Properties Ltd v Dobbs* [2020] NZHC 3494 at [105]. See also the cases referred to above, at para.8-002.

[246] Illustrations 6 and 11; *Concordia Chemische Fabrik auf Actien v Squire* (1876) 34 L.T. 824. But cf. Illustration 12, where the indications in the document were not sufficiently clear.

[247] *Hutcheson v Eaton* (1884) 13 Q.B.D. 861 ("brokers"). As to the term "agent", see *Universal Steam Navigation Co v McKelvie* [1923] A.C. 492, at 501: "When people add 'agent' to a signature to a contract, they are trying to escape personal liability, but are unaware that the attempt will fail". But see Comment to Article 100(1).

[248] Illustrations 1, 2 (first part), 4 and 5.

[249] Illustrations 2 (second part) and 3.

[249a] *Gregor Fisken Ltd v Carl* [2021] EWCA Civ 792; [2021] 4 W.L.R. 91 at [54].

[250] Illustrations 12 and 13. In *Gadd v Houghton* (1876) 1 Ex.D. 357 at 359 James LJ said: "When a man says that he is making a contract 'on account of' someone else, it seems to me that he uses the very strongest terms the English language affords to shew that he is not binding himself, but is binding his principal".

[251] Illustration 14; *Paice v Walker* (1870) L.R. 5 Ex. 173 (but this case was disapproved in *Gadd v*

Houghton (1876) 1 Ex.D. 357); *Weidner v Hoggett* (1876) 1 C.P.D. 533. But such a contingency is unlikely: see *Universal Steam Navigation Co v McKelvie* [1923] A.C. 492 at 499, per Lord Shaw: "But I desire to say that in my opinion the appending of the word 'agents' to the signature of a party to a mercantile contract is, in all cases, the dominating factor in the solution of the problem of principal or agent. A highly improbable and conjectural case (in which this dominating factor might be overcome by other parts of the contract) may by an effort of the imagination be figured, but, apart from that, the appending of the word 'agent' to the signature is a conclusive assertion of agency, and a conclusive rejection of the responsibility of a principal, and is and must be accepted in that twofold sense by the other contracting party".

²⁵² *Southwell v Bowditch* (1876) 1 C.P.D. 374, Illustration 3; *Chartwell Shipping Ltd v Q.N.S. Paper Co Ltd* [1989] 2 S.C.R. 683; (1989) 62 D.L.R. (4th) 36, Illustration 9.

Article 100

ADMISSIBILITY OF EXTRINSIC EVIDENCE

Replace list item "(1)" with:

(1) Where it is clear from the terms of a written contract made by an agent that the agent is contracting personally, extrinsic evidence is not admissible to show that, notwithstanding the terms of the contract, it was the intention of the parties that the agent should not be personally liable on it, because such evidence would be contradictory to the written contract.²⁷⁸   **9-039**

²⁷⁸ *Higgins v Senior* (1841) 8 M. & W. 834, Illustration 1; *Magee v Atkinson* (1837) 2 M. & W. 440; *Sobell Industries v Cory Bros* [1955] 2 Lloyd's Rep. 82 Illustration 7 to Article 98; *Sika Contracts Ltd v B.S. Gill* (1978) 9 Build. L.R. 11, Illustration 10 to Article 99; *Transcontinental Underwriting Agency Srl v General Union Insurance Co Ltd* [1987] 2 Lloyd's Rep. 409; *K v S* [2015] EWHC 1945 (Comm); *Gregor Fisken Ltd v Carl* [2021] EWCA Civ 792; [2021] 4 W.L.R. 91 at [64]. See, further, the cases referred to in para.8-002, above.

ILLUSTRATIONS

Replace list item "(12)" with:

(12) A co-owner of land, A, has express authority to sell land on behalf of both owners, but has no actual authority to make a commission agreement with real estate agent that would bind both owners. A is found to warrant to the real estate agent his authority to engage the agent on behalf of both owners and is liable for the full commission on the sale of the land.⁴⁹¹   **9-083**

⁴⁹¹ *Mathews v CD Realty (PN) Ltd* [2010] NZHC 1881.

COMMENT

Rule (1)

Replace footnote 518 with:

⁵¹⁸ *Rover International Ltd v Cannon Film Sales Ltd* [1987] B.C.L.C. 540; decision varied on other grounds [1989] 1 W.L.R. 912. As to overseas companies, see Overseas Companies (Execution of Documents and Registration of Charges) Regulations 2009, SI 2009/1917.   **9-086**

3. TORTS

COMMENT

Torts connected with contract—deceit and negligent misstatement

Replace footnote 722 with:

⁷²² *Williams v Natural Life Health Foods Ltd* [1998] 1 W.L.R. 830 (HL); and see *NRAM Ltd v Steel*   **9-117**

[2018] UKSC 13; [2018] 1 W.L.R. 1190 (Scot). See also *Gran Gelato Ltd v Richcliff (Group) Ltd* [1992] Ch. 560 at 569; and *Spring v Guardian Assurance Plc* [1995] 2 A.C. 296 at 316, per Lord Goff of Chieveley; *Foster v Action Aviation Ltd* [2014] EWCA Civ 1368 (fact director was beneficial owner of asset being sold by his company not important); *NDH Properties Ltd v Lupton Fawcett LLP* [2020] EWHC 3056 (Ch) at [113]; *Barclay-Watt v Alpha Panareti Public Ltd* [2021] EWHC 1327 (Comm) at [62].

Companies

Replace paragraph with:

9-119   For a short period, it was thought that the position of company directors was different to that of agents in general in relation to torts and other wrongs; they were to be identified with the company and not personally liable.[733] There was, however, no reason to privilege directors over employees and other agents,[734] and it has been affirmed that the general principles applicable to unincorporated principals and their agents are as applicable to companies and directors.[735] Where tortious liability turns on an assumption of responsibility, as in the tort of negligent misstatement, it may be found that directors, like other agents, have not assumed any personal liability, but rather have acted solely on behalf of the company, their principal.[736] Otherwise, directors can be liable in tort in the same way as anyone else. They may, however, be liable for procuring the commission of a tort or other wrong by the company or one of its employees, a subject discussed next. There is some authority that a company may commit the tort of conspiracy by conspiring with its sole director.[737] This is a difficult notion. At the least, it would require that the director (or directors, if more than one is involved) purport to perform some acts necessary for the tort in a personal capacity and not merely as agent of the company, since conspiracy requires not only agreement between two or more persons but acts performed by, or perhaps on behalf of, each of them.[738] Further, if a company were to be a direct party to the common design, as opposed to merely vicariously liable for the acts of others, it would need to be shown that the relevant director had authority to commit the wrongful conduct on the company's behalf.[739]

[733] See *Trevor Ivory Ltd v Anderson* [1992] 2 N.Z.L.R. 517 at 524, 528; *Standard Chartered Bank v Pakistan National Shipping Corp (No.2)* [2000] 1 Lloyd's Rep. 218 CA; reversed [2002] UKHL 43; [2003] 1 A.C. 959.

[734] See above, para.1-029; and Watts (2001) 116 L.Q.R. 525; Flannigan (2002) 81 Can.Bar Rev. 247; Campbell and Armour [2003] C.L.J. 290; Reynolds (2003) 33 H.K.L.J. 51; Stevens [2005] L.M.C.L.Q. 101.

[735] *Standard Chartered Bank v Pakistan National Shipping Corp (No.2)* [2002] UKHL 43; [2003] 1 A.C. 959 (deceit); *Lewis v Yeeles* [2010] EWCA Civ 326 at [26] (procuring a breach of contract by a third party); *Body Corporate 202254 v Taylor* [2009] 2 N.Z.L.R. 17; *Eco3 Capital Ltd v Ludsin Overseas Ltd* [2013] EWCA Civ 413 at [125].

[736] *Williams v Natural Life Health Foods Ltd* [1998] 1 W.L.R. 830; *Foster v Action Aviation Ltd* [2014] EWCA Civ 1368; *PJSC Uralkali v Rowley* [2020] EWHC 3442 (Ch) at [355] (company administrator).

[737] *Barclay Pharmaceuticals Ltd v Waypharm LP* [2012] EWHC 306 (Comm); [2013] 2 B.C.L.C. 551 at [229] (criticised by Watts, in *Agency Law in Commercial Practice* (Busch, Macgregor and Watts eds), pp.108–113); *Raja v McMillan* [2021] EWCA Civ 1103 at [56]. See too *O'Brien v Dawson* (1942) 66 C.L.R. 18 at 32 and 34.

[738] See Carty, *An Analysis of the Economic Torts* (2010), Ch.6; Carty (1999) 19 L.S. 489; and *Uavend Properties Inc v Adsaax Ltd* [2020] EWHC 2073 (Comm) at [94].

[739] As to authority to act illegally, see above, paras 2-026 and 6-023. See also *Digicel (St Lucia) Ltd v Cable & Wireless Plc* [2010] EWHC 774 (Ch), Annex I at [77] (alleged conspiracy as between related companies).

Procuring of, and other involvement in, wrongs

Replace paragraph with:

9-120   Agents, including directors, can be liable for procuring or authorising the commission of torts or other wrongs by others.[740] Again, this is simply part of the general law, and by no means limited to agents. Many of the leading cases, however, have involved directors who have directed more junior agents to do things which are actionable.[741] There are numerous cases on each side of the line in relation to patent and copyright infringement.[742] Where the agent has actually committed the central acts constituting the wrong, thereby making the employer liable, it will not normally be appropriate to plead that the agent has procured the employer to commit the wrong; the agent will be a primary tortfeasor not a secondary one in such cases.[743] It would also be unnecessary, as a rule, to use the concept of procurement where the defendant uttered a fraudulent, or defamatory, statement intending that some other party, innocent or not, would pass on the inaccurate information to the claimant; the utterer would be directly liable in deceit, or defamation.[744] Apart from liability for procurement or authorisation, agents can also find themselves subject to liability for participating in a common design to commit a tort or other wrong.[745] Where there is an intention to injure there is also the possibility of liability in the separate tort of conspiracy.[746] In English law, there is, at present anyway, no concept of merely facilitating the commission of the tort of another.[747]

[740] See *Clerk & Lindsell on Torts* (22nd edn), para.5-79 onwards; Carty (1999) 19 L.S. 489; Stevens, *Torts and Rights* (2007), Ch.7; Davies [2011] C.L.J. 353; Davies, *Accessory Liability* (2015).

[741] e.g. *Yuille v B&B Fisheries (Leigh) Ltd* [1958] 2 Lloyd's Rep. 596 (sending unseaworthy vessels to sea); *Wah Tat Bank Ltd v Chan Cheng Kum* [1975] A.C. 507 (PC) (conversion for delivery of goods without bill of lading); *Anderson Antiques (UK) Ltd v Anderson Wharf (Hull) Ltd* [2007] EWHC 2086 (Ch) (procuring company to wrongly register notices against registered title); *Marex Financial Ltd v Garcia* [2017] EWHC 918 (Comm); [2017] 4 W.L.R. 105 (liability for stripping company of assets to defeat judgment). cf. *Rainham Chemical Works v Belvedere Fish Guano Ltd* [1921] 2 A.C. 465 (no liability for factory explosion); *CBS Songs Ltd v Amstrad Consumer Electronics Plc* [1988] A.C. 1013. As to the concept of "authorising" infringement, see the cases cited in para.8-195; and *Ellis v Sheffield Gas Consumers Co* (1853) 2 E. & B. 767; *Southwark LBC v Mills* [2001] 1 A.C. 1 at 22; *Twentieth Century Fox Film Corp v Newzbin Ltd* [2010] EWHC 608 (Ch); [2010] F.S.R. 21; *Body Corporate 366611 v Wu* [2014] NZSC 137; [2015] 1 N.Z.L.R. 215 (owner of property authorised agent to commit trespass), varied on appeal [2014] NZSC 137; [2015] 1 N.Z.L.R. 215 (liability for trespass); *Twentieth Century Fox Film Corp v Sky UK Ltd* [2015] EWHC 1082 (Ch); cf. *Coventry v Lawrence (No.2)* [2014] UKSC 46; [2015] A.C. 106 (landlord did not authorise nuisance merely by collecting rent from known tortfeasor).

[742] e.g. *Performing Rights Society v Ciryl Theatrical Syndicate Ltd* [1924] 1 K.B. 1; *British Thomson-Houston Co Ltd v Stirling Accessories Ltd* [1924] 2 Ch 33; *Mentmore Manufacturing Co Ltd v National Merchandising Co Ltd* (1978) 89 D.L.R. (3d) 195; *Hoover Plc v George Hulme (Stockport) Ltd* [1992] F.S.R. 565; *White Horse Distillers Ltd v Gregson Associates Ltd* [1984] R.P.C. 61; *C. Evans & Sons Ltd v Spritebrand Ltd* [1985] 1 W.L.R. 317; *PLG Research Ltd v Ardon International Ltd* [1993] F.S.R. 197; *Root Quality Pty Ltd v Root Control Technologies Pty Ltd* (2001) 177 A.L.R. 231; *MCA Records Inc v Charly Records Ltd* [2001] EWCA Civ 1441; [2002] F.S.R. 26; [2003] 1 B.C.L.C. 93; *Societa Esplosivi Industriali Spa v Ordnance Technologies (UK) Ltd* [2007] EWHC 2875 (Ch); [2008] 2 B.C.L.C. 428; *Football Association Premier League Ltd v QC Leisure* [2008] EWHC 1411 (Ch); *JR Consulting & Drafting Pty Ltd v Cummings* [2016] FCAFC 20; *Phonographic Performance Ltd v CGK Trading Ltd* [2016] EWHC 2642 (Ch); *Lifestyle Equities CV v Ahmed* [2021] EWCA Civ 675; [2021] Bus. L.R. 1020 at [41] (and see subsequent judgment at [2021] EWHC 1212 (Ch)). For commentary, see Hon. R. Arnold and P. Davies (2017) 133 L.Q.R. 442.

[743] *Williams v Natural Life Health Foods Ltd* [1998] 1 W.L.R. 830 at 838–839; *Standard Chartered Bank v Pakistan National Shipping Corp (No.2)* [2002] UKHL 43; [2003] 1 A.C. 959 at [38]. cf. *Watson v Dolmark Industries Ltd* [1992] 3 N.Z.L.R. 311.

[744] See, e.g. *Cornfoot v Fowke* (1840) 6 M. & W. 358 at 373–374; *Egger v Viscount Chelmsford* [1965] 1 Q.B. 248 at 261; *Clef Aquitaine Sarl v Laporte Materials (Barrow) Ltd* [2001] Q.B. 488 at 502–503.

[745] *The Koursk* [1924] P. 140; *Brooke v Bool* [1928] 2 K.B. 578; *Unilever Plc v Chefaro* [1994] F.S.R. 135; *Fish & Fish Ltd v Sea Shepherd UK* [2015] UKSC 10; [2015] A.C. 1229 (noted McMeel [2016] L.M.C.L.Q. 29); *Glaxo Wellcome UK Ltd (t/a Allen & Hanburys) v Sandoz Ltd* [2017] EWCA Civ 227; *Tunein Inc v Warner Music UK Ltd* [2021] EWCA Civ 441 at [175]. cf. *Kalma v African Minerals Ltd* [2020] EWCA Civ 144.

[746] See, in general, *Kuwait Oil Tanker Co SAK v Al Bader* [2000] 2 All E.R. (Comm) 271; *OBG Ltd v Allan* [2007] UKHL 21; [2008] 1 A.C. 1; *Meretz Investments NV v ACP Ltd* [2007] EWCA Civ 1303;

[2008] Ch. 244; *Revenue and Customs Commissioners v Total Network SL* [2008] UKHL 19; [2008] A.C. 1174; *JSC BTA Bank v Khrapunov* [2018] UKSC 19; [2018] 2 W.L.R. 1125. For recent cases involving directors and agents, see *Digicel (St Lucia) Ltd v Cable & Wireless Plc* [2010] EWHC 774 (Ch) at Annex I; *Baldwin v Berryland Books* [2010] EWCA Civ 1440; *Stevenson v Singh* [2012] EWHC 2880 (QB) at [18]; *Alpstream AG v PK Airfinance Sarl* [2013] EWHC 2370 (Comm) at [110]; *Emerald Supplies Ltd v British Airways Plc* [2015] EWCA Civ 1024; [2016] Bus. L.R. 145; *Cullen Investments Ltd v Brown* [2017] EWHC 1586 (Ch). cf. Stevens, *Torts and Rights* (2007), Ch.7. P. Davies and Rt Hon. Sir Philip Sales, "Intentional harm, accessories and conspiracies" (2018) 134 L.Q.R. 69.

[747] See, e.g. *Credit Lyonnais v Export Credit Guarantee Department* [1998] 1 Lloyd's Rep. 19; affirmed [2000] 1 A.C. 486; *Fish & Fish Ltd v Sea Shepherd UK* [2015] UKSC 10; [2015] A.C. 1229.

Inducement of breach of contract?

Replace paragraph with:

9-121   In *Said v Butt*[748] it was held that an agent could not be liable for inducing a breach of contract by the principal. A major reason given was that the liability of the principal, for whom the agent acted, and who would be responsible, could not lie in tort but would rather be for breach of contract. This ground is not convincing.[749] It would be equally unconvincing, however, simply to conclude that all torts must be governed by the same rules.[750] The tort of inducing breach of contract is itself problematic, given that deliberate breach of contract does not itself engage the law of tort. Imposing liability on agents for inducing breach of contract would be to place them in an invidious position when their duty is to act in the best interests of their principal and they conclude that breaching the contract is in their principal's interests. Principals should not be disadvantaged because they have employed agents and relied on them to assess their interests.[751] Where the principal is a company, absent the immunity, directors could find themselves personally liable for any deliberate breach of contract that they cause the company to commit.[752] For these reasons the identity of interest between the promisor and its agents is a qualification to the concept of inducement of a breach of contract, not an exception or defence.[753] *Said v Butt* has been followed in later decisions.[754] It may however be possible to claim where the defendant did not purport to act as agent or acted in clear breach of duty to the principal or employer[755] or not in good faith.[756] A shareholder of a company, including a parent company, would not automatically be protected by the agency qualification.[757] But even a parent company can be the agent of a subsidiary if so authorised, and therefore protected by the above principles. In such circumstances, it would seem not to matter that both principal and agent have the same directors, so long as regard is had to the capacity in which they have acted.[758] Even without an agency, a shareholder ought not to be liable for acts of its agents taken in a different capacity, including as directors of a subsidiary.[759] On that basis, it is likely to be rare in practice that a parent company would be liable for the tort of inducement; it is an outsider's wrong.[760] It is also possible for a contract between the parties to exclude the possibility of suit against agents for inducing a breach by any of the parties.[761]

[748] *Said v Butt* [1920] 3 K.B. 497; *Welsh Development Agency v Export Finance Co Ltd* [1992] B.C.L.C. 148 at 171–173, 179–182 and 191. See Oditah [1992] J.B.L. 541 at 565–569; Tan (2011) 23 Sing. Ac. L.J. 816.

[749] See *Welsh Development Agency v Export Finance Co Ltd* [1992] B.C.L.C. 148 at 173, 191.

[750] See in respect of conversion, below para.9-126. The first basis for the decision concerned the doctrine of the undisclosed principal: see above, para.8-079.

[751] See *PT Sandipala Arthaputra v ST Microelectronics Asia Pacific Pte Ltd* [2018] SGCA 17 at [64].

[752] *PT Sandipala Arthaputra v ST Microelectronics Asia Pacific Pte Ltd* [2018] SGCA 17 at [63].

[753] *PT Sandipala Arthaputra v ST Microelectronics Asia Pacific Pte Ltd* [2018] SGCA 17 at [65].

[754] *G. Scammell & Nephew Ltd v Hurley* [1929] 1 K.B. 419 at 443 and 449; *D.C. Thomson & Co Ltd v*

Deakin [1952] Ch. 646 at 680, 681; *O'Brien v Dawson* (1942) 66 C.L.R. 18 at 32, 34; *Rutherford v Poole* [1953] V.L.R. 130 at 135–136; *Official Assignee v Dowling* [1964] N.Z.L.R. 578 at 580–581; *Telemetrix Plc v Modern Engineers of Bristol (Holdings) Plc* [1985] B.C.L.C. 213 at 217; *Holding Oil Finance Inc v Marc Rich & Co AG* [1996] C.L.Y. 1085; *Cook Strait Skyferry Ltd v Dennis Thompson International Ltd* [1993] 2 N.Z.L.R. 72; *Ridgeway Maritime Inc v Beulah Wings Ltd, The Leon* [1991] 2 Lloyd's Rep. 611; *Goodacre v Meyer* [2002] EWHC 1785 (Ch) (no liability for procurement of alleged breach of commission-sharing agreement); *Johnson Matthey (Aust.) Ltd v Dascorp Pty Ltd* (2003) 9 V.R. 171; *Dargaville Farms Ltd v Webster* [2017] NZHC 1790 at [45]. But cf. *Thames Valley Housing Association Ltd v Elegant (Guernsey) Ltd* [2011] EWHC 1288 (Ch) at [110], where, however, *Said v Butt* and the foregoing cases were not referred to. It was suggested therein that the position may be different for directors who are performing their constitutional role in good faith. But, there is, it is submitted, no good reason to protect directors at the expense of employees and other agents who are also attempting to do their best for their principal; they are all immune from action.

[755] See *The Leon* [1991] 2 Lloyd's Rep. 611 at 624–625, per Waller J; *SPL Private Finance (PF1) IC Ltd v Arch Financial Products LLP* [2014] EWHC 4268 (Comm) at [288]; *Antuzis v DJ Houghton Catching Services Ltd* [2019] EWHC 843 (QB); [2019] Bus. L.R. 1532 (a difficult decision involving judicial review of directors' decision-making and applying an inapt analogy to the position in deceit, where agents will always be liable). See also *Official Assignee v Dowling* [1964] N.Z.L.R. 578 at 580–581; *Clerk & Lindsell on Torts* (22nd edn), para.24-36.

[756] *Official Assignee v Dowling* [1964] N.Z.L.R. 578 at 580–581; *Bromley Industries Ltd v Martin & Judith Fitzsimons Ltd* [2009] NZHC 1992; *Knights Capital Group Ltd v Bajada and Associates Pty Ltd* [2016] WASC 69 at [76]; *Turf Club Emporium Pte Ltd v Yeo Boong Hua* [2018] SGCA 44 at [316].

[757] See *Esso Petroleum Co Ltd v Kingswood Motors (Addleston) Ltd* [1974] Q.B. 142 at 155; *Stocznia Gdanska SA v Latvian Shipping Co (No.3)* [2002] EWCA Civ 889; [2002] 2 All E.R. (Comm) 768; [2002] 2 Lloyd's Rep. 436 (parent company liable for inducing subsidiary's breach) (noted by Edmundson (2008) 30 M.U.L.R. 62); *Lewis v Yeeles* [2010] EWCA Civ 326 at [26] (director of third party company not immune from personal liability for inducing breach of contract by a fourth party). But cf. *Bumi Armada Offshore Holdings Ltd v Tozzi Srl* [2018] SGCA(I) 05, per Lord Neuberger IJ (noted P Koh (2020) 136 L.Q.R. 30; Lau Kwan Ho [2020] L.M.C.L.Q. 13).

[758] *LMI Australasia Pty Ltd v Baulderstone Hornibrook Pty Ltd* [2003] NSWCA 74; *Bumi Armada Offshore Holdings Ltd v Tozzi Srl* [2018] SGCA(I) 05; *Uavend Properties Inc v Adsaax Ltd* [2020] EWHC 2073 (Comm) at [69] and [79].

[759] See *Kuwait Asia Bank EC v National Mutual Life Nominees Ltd* [1991] 1 A.C. 187 (PC) at 221–222; *Bumi Armada Offshore Holdings Ltd v Tozzi Srl* [2018] SGCA(I) 05.

[760] See *O'Brien v Dawson* (1941) 41 S.R.(N.S.W.) 295 at 307–308; affirmed (1942) 66 C.L.R. 18 at 32 and 34: wrongdoers have to be "*outsiders*" who are influencing the independent volition of a contracting party who is capable of exercising volition for himself".

[761] *Mir Steel UK Ltd v Morris* [2012] EWCA Civ 1397 at [39].

4. EQUITY

COMMENT

Rule (1): Accessory liability in respect of breach of trust

To the end of the first paragraph, add:

Sometimes it may be possible for the principal to sue the agent on behalf of the third-party victim in order to cure the breach of duty in which the agent caused the principal to engage.[851a]   **9-135**

[851a] See the cases cited in para.8-214, above.

Replace footnote 853 with:

[853] See *Bilta (UK) Ltd v Natwest Markets Plc* [2020] EWHC 546 (Ch) at [162]–[165], [174], revsd on other points, *Natwest Markets Plc v Bilta (UK) Ltd* [2021] EWCA Civ 680 at [134].

Replace footnote 867 with:

[867] *Barlow Clowes International Ltd v Eurotrust Ltd* [2005] UKPC 37; [2006] 1 All E.R. 333 at [15], per Lord Hoffmann; see Yeo (2006) 122 L.Q.R. 171. See also *US International Marketing Ltd v National Bank of New Zealand Ltd* [2004] 1 N.Z.L.R. 589; *Central Bank of Ecuador v Conticorp SA* [2015] UKPC 11; [2016] 1 B.C.L.C. 26 at [9]; *Ivey v Genting Casinos (UK) Ltd* [2017] UKSC 67; [2018] A.C. 391 (noted M. Dyson, "Poison Ivey or herbal tea leaf?" (2018) 134 L.Q.R. 198); *Wingate v Solicitors*

Regulation Authority [2018] EWCA Civ 366; [2018] 1 W.L.R. 3969 (want of integrity); *Natwest Markets Plc v Bilta (UK) Ltd* [2021] EWCA Civ 680 at [130]. Dishonesty is not required for liability for assistance in Australia: *Harstedt Pty Ltd v Tomanek* [2018] VSCA 84.

Replace the fourth paragraph with:
The remedy available to a successful claimant, while sometimes said to treat the defendant as a constructive trustee, is in fact an in personam one for compensation in monetary terms. This category of constructive trusteeship:

> "is nothing more than a formula for equitable relief. The court is saying that the defendant shall be liable in equity as though he were a trustee".[871]

It is calculated by reference to equity's willingness to restore fully funds that can be shown to have suffered a loss by reason of the breach. This could perhaps include profits made by the wrongdoer,[872] but not profits earned only by the principal.[872a] Contributory negligence should not be relevant.[873] Where there are several wrongdoers, each is liable for the full loss, subject to the requirements of contribution inter se under the Civil Liability (Contribution) Act 1978,[874] which need not take account of the relative gravity of fault but may be affected by the continuing existence of the profit in the hands of some parties.[875] It seems possible that the reasoning of the leading House of Lords decision on equitable compensation for breach of trust, *Target Holdings Ltd v Redferns*,[876] will provide a guide. Despite this more generous measure than the common law provides, however, it would seem that the liability has totally outgrown its origin in the law of trusts. It bears little or no resemblance to a constructive trust as regards the requirements for liability or the remedy available for breach. Even Lord Nicholls in his judgment in the Privy Council spoke of the liability as involving a "duty of care".[877] The relationship of this liability to the tort of interference with contract remains open to argument and possibly development.[878]

---

[871] *Selangor United Rubber Estates Ltd v Cradock (No.3)* [1968] 1 W.L.R. 1555 at 1582, per Ungoed-Thomas J; see further *Dubai Aluminium Co Ltd v Salaam* [2002] UKHL 48; [2003] 2 A.C. 366 at [140]–[142], per Lord Millett. For limitation issues applicable to claims against accessories to a breach of trust or fiduciary obligation, see *Williams v Central Bank of Nigeria* [2014] UKSC 10; [2014] A.C. 1189. See too *Halton International Inc v Guernroy Ltd* [2006] EWCA Civ 801.

[872] See Article 96; *Fyffes Group Ltd v Templeman* [2000] 2 Lloyd's Rep. 643 (bribes: see above, para.8-222); *Ultraframe (UK) Ltd v Fielding* [2005] EWHC 1638 (QB) at [1594]; *Novoship (UK) Ltd v Nikitin* [2014] EWCA Civ 908; [2015] 1 Q.B. 499 at [84] (noted Davies (2015) 131 L.Q.R. 173, Gummow [2015] C.L.J. 405); *Central Bank of Ecuador v Conticorp SA* [2015] UKPC 11; [2016] 1 B.C.L.C. 26 addendum at [9]; *Ancient Order of Foresters in Victoria Friendly Society Ltd v Lifeplan Australia Friendly Society Ltd* [2018] HCA 43. But cf. *Royal Brunei Airlines Sdn Bhd v Tan* [1995] 2 A.C. 378 at 386 (accessory liability not restitution based). See further, para.8-225.

[872a] *Lifestyle Equities CV v Ahmed* [2021] EWCA Civ 675; [2021] Bus. L.R. 1020 at [17].

[873] See *Corporacion Nacional del Cobre de Chile v Sogemin Metals Ltd* [1997] 1 W.L.R. 1396; *Standard Chartered Bank v Pakistan National Shipping Corp (No.2)* [2002] UKHL 43; [2003] 1 A.C. 959.

[874] See above, para.8-191.

[875] *Dubai Aluminium Co Ltd v Salaam* [2002] UKHL 48; [2003] 2 A.C. 366. It has been held that there is no necessary inconsistency between a party's being liable in knowing receipt of a claimant's funds and that party having a right of contribution under the Civil Liability (Contribution) Act 1978 against the agents (including directors) of the claimant who caused the misapplication of the funds. The court, however, left open the issue whether the liability would be for the "same damage" within s.1(1): *City Index Ltd v Gawler* [2007] EWCA Civ 1382; [2008] 3 All E.R. 126.

[876] *Target Holdings Ltd v Redferns* [1996] A.C. 421; *Group Seven Ltd v Notable Services LLP* [2019] EWCA Civ 614; [2020] Ch. 129 at [110]. See para.6-043.

[877] *Target Holdings Ltd v Redferns* [1995] 2 A.C. at 391–339.

[878] In *Metall und Rohstoff AG v Donaldson Lufkin & Jenrette Inc* [1990] 1 Q.B. 391 at 481 the Court of Appeal rejected the existence of a tort of procuring a breach of trust. See however the Rt Hon. Lord Hoffmann in *The Frontiers of Liability* (Birks ed., 1994), Vol.1, p.28. A claim under this head was held

to lie in "tort, delict or quasi-delict" for the purposes of art.5(3) of the Brussels Convention on Jurisdiction and the Enforcement of Judgments in *Casio Computer Co Ltd v Sayo* [2001] EWCA Civ 661; [2001] I.L.Pr. 43; see also *Grupo Torras SA v Al Sabbah (No.5)* [2001] Lloyd's Rep. Bank 36. cf. *OBG Ltd v Allan* [2007] UKHL 21; [2008] 1 A.C. 1 at [192] and [202].

Rule (2): Receipt of trust property

After the first paragraph, add new paragraph:

9-136 One problematic situation where a knowing receipt action may arise against an agent is where it is alleged that the agent's own remuneration was paid by the principal out of the third party's assets. While in principle the agent could be liable in such circumstances, case law also suggests that the agent may avoid liability where the remuneration was earned in good faith helping the principal, with some colour of right, defend the claimant's assertions of a proprietary interest in the assets in question.[879a]

[879a] See *Carl Zeiss Stiftung v Herbert Smith & Co (No. 2)* [1969] 2 Ch. 276, Illustration 4 to Article 116; *Re Smith; Serious Fraud Office v Litigation Capital Ltd* [2021] EWHC 1272 (Comm) at [468]; *London Capital & Finance Plc v Thomson* [2021] EWHC 1833 (Ch) at [31]; *Break Fast Investments Pty Ltd v Rigby Cooke Lawyers (A Firm)* [2021] VSC 398 at [297].

Replace the fourth paragraph with:

Most of the modern cases have involved breaches of duty by agents, rather than trustees in the strict sense. In such circumstances, if the recipient cannot establish that the agent had apparent authority liability will usually follow.[891] The position is more complex where the breach is merely of an equitable duty; for some breaches, such as where the contract is affected by a mere conflict of interest, it may be necessary for the claimant to be able to rescind the contract with the recipient before any liability arises.[892] The property must be subject to an equitable interest in the claimant's favour at the moment of receipt, and the disposition itself must involve a breach of trust or breach of fiduciary duty.[893] The position is likely to be different where the defendant owed fiduciary obligations to the claimant and the assets in question are affected by the business-opportunities doctrine. Knowing receipt may not be available in such circumstances, but the defendant will still be accountable and may indeed be a constructive trustee of particular assets.[893a] The measure of liability in knowing receipt is sometimes described as that of a constructive trustee,[894] but again the action is in effect in personam for the replacement of the value lost. It matters not that the receiver has paid it away. It is therefore not clear whether it should include profits made from the property.

[891] *Thanakharn Kasikorn Thai Chamchat v Akai Holdings Ltd (In Liquidation)* (2010) 13 HKCFAR 479 at [136]; *McFee v Reilly* [2019] NSWCA 322 (benefiting from abuse of lasting power of attorney). See Conaglen and Nolan (2013) 129 L.Q.R. 359.

[892] See further above, paras 8-219–8-221.

[893] See *Courtwood Holdings SA v Woodley Properties Ltd* [2018] EWHC 2163 (Ch) at [61].

[893a] See above, para.6-081. The *Courtwood* case, above, arguably gave insufficient weight to the principles of the business-opportunities doctrine.

[894] See *Thanakharn Kasikorn Thai Chamchat v Akai Holdings Ltd (In Liquidation)* (2010) 13 HKCFAR 479 at [156].

Solicitors

After "connection with fiduciaries.", add:

9-140 The cases show a reluctance to make solicitors liable in knowing receipt for their fees earned in defending in good faith a contested claim made against a client alleged to have acted in breach of trust.[916a]

916a See para.9-136, above.

CHAPTER 10

TERMINATION OF AUTHORITY

Article 117

TERMINATION OF ACTUAL AUTHORITY

Replace list item "(1) (a) (b) (c) (d) (e) (f)" with:

(1) The actual authority of an agent is terminated—   **10-002**
    (a) by agreement between principal and agent;
    (b) if given for a particular transaction, by the completion of that transac-
tion[2];
    (c) if given for a limited period, by the expiration of that period, or in any
case after the elapsing of a period which is reasonable in all the circumstances[3];
    (d) by the happening of any event upon the happening of which it is agreed
between the principal and the agent that the authority shall terminate,[4] or
upon the happening of which the agent should reasonably infer that the
principal does not or would not wish the authority to continue[5];
    (e) by the destruction of the subject-matter of the agency[6];
    (f) by the happening of any event rendering the agency or its objects unlaw-
ful, impossible or otherwise frustrating the agency or its objects.[7]

---

[2] Illustrations 1–4.

[3] Illustration 5; *Danby v Coutts & Co* (1885) 29 Ch.D. 550, Illustration 1 to Article 24.

[4] See *Restatement, Third*, § 3.09.

[5] See Comment. Mere cessation of the agent's business does not of itself terminate his authority: *Triffit Nurseries v Salads Etcetera Ltd* [1999] 1 All E.R. (Comm) 110; [2000] 1 All E.R. (Comm) 737. cf. *Angove's Pty Ltd v Bailey* [2016] UKSC 47; [2016] 1 W.L.R. 3179.

[6] *Rhodes v Forwood* (1876) 1 App.Cas. 256, Illustration 1 to Article 123; *Northey v Trevillion* (1902) 7 Com.Cas. 201. See Article 123.

[7] See Comment.

COMMENT

Rule (1)

Replace the first paragraph with:

10-003   The circumstances stated in Rule (1) above are relevant to the agreement, whether contractual or not, between principal and agent, and relate to implied (or express) terms of it. They are no more than illustrations of situations in which the agent is not justified in thinking that authority continues. The fact that a principal grants more than one power of attorney (whether to different agents or to the same agent) does not necessarily indicate that the principal intended that earlier powers are revoked.[10a] It should also be noted that even where revocation occurs the third party may still be able to rely in some cases on the doctrine of apparent authority.[11] The propositions contained in (a)–(c) are self-evident. The second part of (d) is derived from a suggestion in *Restatement, Third*[12] that circumstances may occur in which at the time the directed act was to be performed it is no longer reasonable for the agent to believe that the principal would wish the agent to do so. Where however the agent is in reasonable doubt as to whether authority persists, the agent's actions are to be treated as authorised if reasonable in the circumstances.[13] Rule (1)(e) is again self-evident for cases where a subject-matter can be readily identified, though here the correct analysis of the contractual position, and hence whether the principal is liable to the agent, is open to much argument.[14] In both these cases it is a matter of interpretation whether the actual authority ends on the happening of the event or on the agent's receiving notice of the happening of the event.

[10a] *Re E* [2001] Ch. 364 at [22]; *Broadway Plaza Investments Pty Ltd v Broadway Plaza Pty Ltd* [2020] NSWSC 1778 at [2215].

[11] See Article 121.

[12] See Comment *b* to § 3.06.

[13] cf. Articles 26 and 38.

[14] See Article 123.

COMMENT

Reference to irrevocable authority in other contexts

(4)   Third party's contractual right to serve notices or make payments to named agent

Replace footnote 108 with:

10-010   [108] See *DVB Bank SE v Isim Amin Ltd* [2014] EWHC 2156 (Comm) at [5]; *Citicorp Trustee Co Ltd v Al-Sanea* [2017] EWHC 2845 (Comm) at [33]; *Royal Petrol Trading Co UK v Total India Pvt Ltd* [2018] EWHC 1272 (Comm) at [40]; *Bank of New York Mellon, London Branch v Essar Steel India Ltd* [2018] EWHC 3177 (Ch) at [16]; *Barclays Bank Plc v Al Saud* [2021] EWHC 701 (Comm) at [4].

COMMERCIAL AGENTS

2. THE COMMERCIAL AGENTS REGULATIONS

Interpretation

To the end of the second paragraph, add new footnote 22a:

11-004

[22a] See a useful article by S. Whittaker, "Retaining European Union Law in the United Kingdom" (2021) 136 L.Q.R. 477.

CONFLICT OF LAWS

INTRODUCTION

The internal law: the Rome I Regulation

Replace footnote 16 with:

[16] Article 4.4. In *GDE LLC v Anglia Autoflow Ltd* [2020] EWHC 105 (Comm); [2020] 1 W.L.R. 2381, **12-003** a case governed by the Rome Convention, the provisions of which are somewhat different in this respect, the court fell back on the equivalent of Article 4.4 and applied the law of closest connection where an agent who might have been held to effect the characteristic performance was not in existence (because not incorporated) on the date of the agency agreement.

INDEX

Chitty on Contracts 34th edition

Hugh Beale

ISBN: 9780414098251

Publication date: October 2021

Formats: Hardback/ProView eBook/Westlaw UK

The leading reference work on contract law in the Common Law world. Chitty offers guidance to the whole range of contract law as practiced in the UK. New developments include coverage of all the latest relevant case law, an expanded chapter on Restrictive Agreements and Competition, an updated account of the effects of Brexit on contracts, and the implications of the Trade and Cooperation Agreement.

The Law of Personal Property 3rd edition

Michael Bridge, Louise Gullifer, Gerard McMeel, Kelvin F.K Low

ISBN: 9780414098152

Publication date: November 2021

Formats: Hardback/ProView eBook/Westlaw UK

Issues and disputes concerning personal property are a common feature of commercial legal practice. The new edition of this authoritative guide provides comprehensive, in-depth treatment of both tangible and intangible personal property. Key changes include a new chapter on Digital Assets, substantially extended treatment of electronic documentation, and a discussion of the impact of Brexit.

Formation and Variation of Contracts 3rd edition

John Cartwright

ISBN: 9780414090705

Publication date: August 2021

Formats: Hardback/ProView eBook/Westlaw UK

This work deals with topics fundamental to the question of enforceability of promises made and how contracting parties can ensure their transaction is legally effective. The significance of the UK's withdrawal from the EU is covered, as are changes in topics such as pre-contractual negotiations, electronic signatures, contract formalities, "no oral modification" clauses, and consideration.

Contact us: *Tel: +44 (0)345 600 9355*   *Order online: sweetandmaxwell.co.uk*